Mrs Robert Peffer

To my dear Sister

May this book be an inspiration to you. God bless you & keep you.

Love Evelyn

GOD MADE THE VIOLET TOO

"A violet by a mossy stone
Half hidden from the eye;
Fair as a star, when only one
Is shining in the sky."

(From Wordsworth's "She Dwelt Among the Untrodden Ways")

God Made The Violet Too

Life of Leonie,
Sister of St. Therese

REV. ALBERT H. DOLAN, O. Carm.

THE CARMELITE PRESS

6413 Dante Avenue
Chicago 37, Illinois

55 Demarest Avenue
Englewood, New Jersey

Nihil obstat *Imprimi potest*

The Very Rev. MATTHEW O'NEILL, *O. Carm.*
Provincial and Censor Librorum

Imprimatur

+ SAMUEL CARDINAL STRITCH
Archbishop of Chicago

June 9, 1948.

First Printing, 1948

CONTENTS

Chapter		Page
ONE	*Introductory. The Little Flower's Summary of Leonie's Life*	3
TWO	*Birth. Infancy. Childhood, until the Death of Her Mother When Leonie Was Fourteen*	11
THREE	*Adolescence, from the Age of Fourteen to Eighteen. Sponsor for Therese. Finishes School*	39
FOUR	*Tries Religious Life Three Times and Fails Each Time. From the Age of Twenty-three to Thirty-four. Death of Therese*	48
FIVE	*Final Entrance of Leonie at Thirty-six. Earlier Years in Religion. Characteristics*	60
SIX	*The Rose Blooms. The Humble Violet Hides. Leonie during the Years of the Glorification of Therese*	73
SEVEN	*Homesickness for Heaven. Other Characteristics and Virtues. Holy Death*	92

LIST OF ILLUSTRATIONS

	PAGE
Mrs. Martin, Leonie's Mother - - -	29
Mr. Martin, Leonie's Father - - - -	41
Isadore Guerin, Leonie's Uncle - - -	54
Mrs. Isadore Guerin, Leonie's Aunt - -	57
Marie Guerin, Leonie's Cousin - - -	66
Leonie's Handwriting - - - - -	100
Leonie and her Four Sisters - - - -	107
Leonie at Thirty-two - - - - -	111
Leonie in 1915 - - - - - -	116
Family Group - - - - - -	119

CHAPTER ONE

INTRODUCTORY. THE LITTLE FLOWER'S SUMMARY OF LEONIE'S LIFE.

This is the story of a nun who entered and left the convent three times; the fourth time she persevered in the religious life and for forty-two years lived in the convent, where now the Sisters venerate her and pray to her as to a saint. It is the story of Leonie Martin, the sister of St. Therese.

If St. Therese may be compared to a rose in full bloom, so Leonie may be compared to a violet "half hidden from the eye." St. Therese herself might be said to have written the life of Leonie when she penned these lines of the first chapter of her *Autobiography*:

"I often asked myself why God has preferences, why all souls do not receive an equal measure of grace. I was filled with wonder when I saw extraordinary favours showered on sinners such as St. Paul, St. Augustine, St. Mary Magdalen, and so many others whom He forced, so to speak, to receive His grace. In reading the lives of the Saints, I was surprised to see there were certain privileged souls whom Our Lord favoured from the cradle to the grave, allowing no obstacle in their path which might keep them from mounting towards Him, and preventing sin from soiling the spotless brightness of their baptismal robe. And again it puzzled me why so many poor savages should die without having even heard the name of God.

"Our Lord has deigned to explain to me this mystery. He showed me the book of Nature, and I understood that every flower created by Him is beautiful, that the brilliance of the rose and the whiteness of the lily do not lessen the perfume of the violet or the sweet simplicity of the daisy. I understood that if all the lowly flowers wished to be roses, Nature would lose her springtide beauty, and the fields would no longer be enamelled with lovely hues.

"It is the same in the world of souls, Our Lord's living garden. He has been pleased to create great Saints who may be compared to the lily and the rose; but He has also created lesser ones, who must be content to be daisies or simple violets flowering at His feet, and whose mission is to gladden His divine eyes when He deigns to look down upon them: the more joyfully they do His will, the greater is their perfection.

"I understand this also, that God's love is made manifest as well in a simple soul which does not resist His grace as in one more highly endowed."

In that passage St. Therese gives us, in effect, a summary of the life of Leonie, and we shall see that the humble violet of the blessed garden of the Martin family had fragrance, special grace and beauty of its own, and reveals very eloquently the wondrous workmanship of its Creator. God made the violet too.

This life of Leonie has been written for several reasons. First, because the devotees of St. Therese love to penetrate into the intimacy of the inner sanctuary of the Martin family, to be edified by the examples of solid virtue revealed to us there. Entering their home, we understand better the providential environment which produced a saint.

Particularly will parents, for whom also this book is written, be impressed by the example of the Martin household. If Christian society is to be reformed, the family cell must be regenerated and impregnated with faith. The glory of St. Therese redounds upon her holy parents, for she was, as is normal, the fruit and the reward of their life. The essential task of parents in collaborating with God is to train their children for heaven, since human existence has no other purpose than to lead to heaven. Blessed are the fathers and mothers who are associates in this noble task and who have the happiness of meeting their children again in heaven where they will be their crowns of glory.

This book will have a special interest for those parents with "problem children," for Leonie in her earlier years caused her holy mother much worry. We shall see how Mrs. Martin devoted herself with loving and sometimes anguished solicitude to the reformation of Leonie's difficult character, given to conflicts and contrasts, but redeemed by a heart of gold. It was the prayers, the persevering efforts and the heroic sacrifices of this admirable mother that obtained for her dear Leonie the grace of becoming finally a well-adjusted person and a holy religious. I cannot imagine a mother who could read Leonie's life without being filled with admiration for Leonie's mother.

All readers will, I believe, be better for having known Leonie, who never entirely exasperates, frequently amuses and finally edifies us and inspires our love. Incidentally, the many who have striven unsuccessfully to enter the religious life will learn from Leonie that it is possible, if not probable, to become a holy religious after having been at first judged unfit for that life.

My sources for this life of Leonie are four: (1) my own prolonged conversations with her in 1926 and 1927; (2) my talks with her Carmelite sisters about her, the last of these visits being in 1947; (3) references to Leonie which have appeared from time to time in *Les Annales de Saint Therese de Lisieux;* (4) finally, the circular letter concerning Leonie distributed in 1941 by the Visitation Convent of Caen where Leonie died. Since this is not a document written for scholars, I have deemed it wise not to clutter these pages with footnotes and references to these four sources but simply to indicate them, once and for all, in this introductory chapter.

Those not too well acquainted with the family of St. Therese will find the following explanatory table useful:

Characters and Places

Mr. Louis Martin: The father of St. Therese. He was born in 1823, married in 1858 and died in 1894.

Mrs. Louis Martin: The mother of St. Therese. Her maiden name was Zelie Guerin. Mrs. Martin was born in 1831 and died in August, 1877. Her brother, Isadore, is the Mr. Guerin of this book. Isadore's wife was Celine Fournet, and as Mrs. Guerin she became a close friend of Mr. and Mrs. Martin.

Sister Marie-Dosithee: The sister of Mrs. Martin. Her name before entering the convent was Louise Guerin. She was a Visitation nun, teaching at Le Mans. She died in February, 1877.

Marie Martin: First daughter of the Martin family, born in February, 1860, died in January, 1940.

Pauline Martin: Second daughter, born in September, 1861, still living.

Leonie Martin: Third daughter, born in June, 1863, died in June, 1941.

Marie-Helene Martin: Fourth daughter, born in October, 1864, died in February, 1870.

Two Martin sons: Born between 1865 and 1867. Both died in infancy.

Celine Martin: Seventh Martin child, born in April, 1869, still living.

Marie-Melanie Martin: Eighth Martin child, born in 1870, died in infancy.

Therese Martin: Ninth Martin child, born in 1873, died in 1897.

Mr. and Mrs. Guerin: See Mrs. Louis Martin.

Marie Guerin: Younger daughter of Isadore and Celine Guerin. Cousin of St. Therese. Born in 1876. Entered Carmel as Sister Marie of the Eucharist. Died in 1905.

Jeanne Guerin: Older daughter of Isadore and Celine Guerin. Cousin of St. Therese. Born in 1868. Married Dr. La Neele. Died in 1938.

Louise Marais: A servant in the Martin home.

Alencon: Town in Normandy in which all the Martin children were born and lived until after the mother's death in 1877.

Lisieux: Town in Normandy to which the Martins moved in 1877. Lisieux is the seat of the Carmelite Convent which four of the Martin children (Pauline, Marie, Celine and Therese) entered.

Buissonnets: The villa or home of the Martins in Lisieux. It means "The Elms" or "The Thickets." The word suggests a mass of honeysuckle, hawthorn, hazels and elms.

Paray-le-Monial: See "The Visitation" below.

Le Mans: A town in Normandy which was the seat of the Visitation Convent School where Marie and Pauline (and for a time, Leonie) were educated. Mrs. Martin's sister, Sister Marie-Dosithee, was a teacher in that school.

Seez (Sees): A town in Normandy which was the seat of a Shrine of Our Lady to which the Martins made several pilgrimages.

Caen: A town in Normandy in which was situated the Visitation Convent which Leonie entered and where she died.

The Visitation: A religious order founded by St. Francis de Sales (1567-1622) in collaboration with St. Jane de Chantal (1572-1641). St. Margaret Mary Alacoque (1647-1690), the apostle of devotion to the Sacred Heart, was a Visitation nun at Paray-le-Monial, in central France, where Our Lord appeared to her and inspired her to establish the "nine First Fridays." St. Margaret Mary was beatified in 1864, but not canonized until 1920.

Process: The inquiry into the virtues of a person proposed for beatification or canonization is called a Process. This Process may be diocesan or Roman. The latter is also called Apostolic. In the case of St. Therese, the Diocesan Process was held in 1910 in Lisieux and Bayeux; the Apostolic Process was held in Lisieux in 1915.

Our Cover: The violets on our cover need no further explanation. The rosary recalls Leonie's devotion to Mary in general and to Mary's rosary in particular.

CHAPTER TWO

BIRTH. INFANCY. CHILDHOOD, UNTIL THE DEATH OF HER MOTHER, WHEN LEONIE WAS FOURTEEN.

Leonie was the third of nine children given by God to Mr. and Mrs. Martin. Marie and Pauline were the first two. Born June 3, 1863, Leonie was baptized the next day, Corpus Christi, a coincidence that always rejoiced the heart of Leonie, profoundly devoted to the Holy Eucharist. We shall see that it was on this same feast that she received her passport to heaven, through the Sacrament of Extreme Unction.

Leonie was a little, blonde baby with blue eyes, and very frail, contrasting sharply with her two older sisters, Marie and Pauline, who were brunettes and full of life. Mrs. Martin wrote to her brother, Isadore Guerin, in March, 1864: "Little Leonie is over nine months old and is not nearly so steady on her feet as Marie was at three months. The poor child is very delicate. She has a sort of chronic whooping cough, happily less violent than that which attacked Pauline, for the good God gives her only as much as she can bear."

In May, 1864, we find the mother writing to her brother: "Little Leonie is not thriving; she does not seem to want to walk. She is extremely small and thin, very feeble and undersized. She has just had the measles and has been very ill, even having violent convulsions."

It was at this time, 1864, that her father undertook on foot a pilgrimage to Notre Dame of Seez to obtain the cure of Leonie. Her parents prayed: "If Leonie is to become a saint one day, cure her." Nevertheless, she remained weak and subject to many illnesses. In March of the following year, the symptoms of ill health increased: continual palpitations, intestinal inflammation. Then came running eczema which spread over her body and reduced her to a pitiable condition.

For sixteen months the child hovered between life and death, and finally Mrs. Martin wrote to her sister, Sister Marie-Dosithee, begging her to make a novena to Blessed Margaret Mary for Leonie. This time, prayer was answered and three months later the mother wrote: "Leonie is very pretty and stronger. It is certainly a fact that she has not been sick since the novena my sister made to Blessed Margaret Mary."

But although her health improved, the child retained, in addition to physical handicaps, other deficiencies; her intelligence developed very slowly and, above all, her character was at once wild and shy, capricious and odd.

In a letter to her brother on April 28, 1865, Mrs. Martin writes: "I love the less pretty one, Leonie, as much as the others, although she will not do me much credit." Leonie was to falsify this prophecy and eventually enrich her mother's crown by her virtues.

Imploring the grace of Leonie's cure, her parents had said to Our Lady: "If she is to become a saint, cure her." That prayer was heard, but laboriously the parents had to educate Leonie's unstable nature, before the mother could write, when Leonie was five: "She seems at present to have as good a character as one would want to see."

From the time that Leonie was old enough to go to school, she was remarkable rather for indifference and wasting time than for docility and attention. She herself in later years frankly admitted that she had been a very poor pupil; in fact, referring to her early school days she humbly used the doubtless somewhat exaggerated phrase, "my detestable childhood." As she grew older, it became evident that she was less favorably endowed than Marie and Pauline. She showed herself to be completely frolicsome, drawing no profit from her studies, her mind fixed instead on amusing herself and plaguing her little fellow-pupils. Understanding nothing of arithmetic, she contented herself with lining up figures haphazardly, one under another, to the desolation of her teacher. She thoroughly resented all attempts at instruction, though her mother endeavored to give her the same education as her older sisters, Marie and Pauline, who were educated at the Visitation Convent at Le Mans under the eye of Mrs. Martin's sister, Sister Marie-Dosithee.

Leonie had a rebellious nature, resisting both restraint and persuasive arguments. A certain mental backwardness and physical deficiency, caused by an uninterrupted succession of illnesses, had hindered her development and an inferiority complex had further helped to produce a child whom it was impossible to govern and almost impossible to understand.

Leonie's taciturnity disconcerted and troubled her mother. She knew the temptations of a soul hermetically sealed, the danger of being driven back upon oneself. Her letters show how she applied herself to know all her children thoroughly, so as to treat each soul according to its needs. Would that every mother in the world could read these letters. She wrote to her brother in July, 1872: "This poor child makes me very anxious, for her character is undisciplined and her intelligence under-developed. . . . I cannot analyze her character; moreover the most learned would be at their wits' end. I hope, all the same, that some day the good seed will spring up. If I see that, I shall sing my *Nunc dimittis.*"

Cheering Prediction by Leonie's Aunt

Mrs. Martin counted heavily upon the pedagogical talents and virtues of her sister at Le Mans, but a first trial of Leonie as a boarder failed lamentably. The child was too capricious to submit to school discipline, too excitable to adapt herself to the common life, and too backward to follow the normal school course. Yet the same aunt was by no means pessimistic. Under the unprepossessing surface, she discerned the germs of solid qualities, and wrote to that effect to Leonie's mother:

"She is a difficult child to train, and her childhood will not show any attractiveness, but I believe that eventually she will be as good as her sisters. She has a heart of gold, her intelligence is not developed and she is backward for her age. Nevertheless, she does not lack capabilities, and I find that she has good judgment and also remarkable strength of character. . . . In short, by nature she is strong and generous, quite to my taste. But if the grace of God were not there, what would become of her?"

Thus this religious teacher had sufficient wisdom to discern the hidden worth of little Leonie's character, and the future fully confirmed the Sister's prediction.

The mother received this prediction joyfully, but in the immediate present the child, whom her aunt called "the child of destiny," and who she sometimes thought might join her in the convent, seemed rather a "bundle of thorns." The death of her sister Helene, who was one year younger than Leonie, had deprived her of the gentle companionship which might have aided in her development. She had private lessons but scarcely seemed to profit by them. Neither reproofs nor caresses had any lasting effect upon her strange character. Her good moments were few and her amendments short-lived.

In January, 1874, in order to prepare the child for her First Communion, her parents gave her another trial at the Visitation. At first it seemed promising. Sister Marie-Dosithee took Leonie under her special care. After a few days, seeing that corrections simply glided off this unstable nature, she changed her tactics and began a system of kindness and perfect confidence. The effect was magical. For a few weeks there seemed reason to think that the battle was won, then all the hopes were shattered. The natural defects returned more violently than ever, accompanied by inattention and unruly behavior.

In April it was necessary to inform the poor mother, who came to fetch her daughter. She made no attempt to obtain another chance, for she held that "when children are difficult, it is for their parents to have the trouble of them." But her disappointment was not the less painful.

"As you may think," she writes June 1, 1874, to Mrs. Guerin, "this has much upset me; it is not too much to say that it has caused deep grief which will be lasting. My one hope of reforming this child lay in my sister, and I was persuaded that they would keep her. But despite the best will in the world, it was necessary to separate her from the rest of the children. As soon as she is with companions, she seems to lose control of herself, and you never saw anything like her unruliness. Well, I have no longer any hope of changing her nature, save by a miracle. It is true that I do not deserve a miracle, but I am hoping against all hope. The more difficult she seems, the more I am persuaded that God will not let her remain like this. I will pray so hard that He will grant my petition. At eighteen months, she was cured of a malady from which she should have died; why did God save her from death if He had not merciful designs for her?"

Leonie's First Holy Communion

The rebellious child had become at one and the same time—mothers will easily understand this paradox—her greatest source of suffering, her chief worry and the object of her most tender affection. She herself prepared Leonie for her First Communion, helped her to learn her catechism, encouraged her to make little sacrifices and, to bring added blessing to her preparation for the ceremony, took her on pilgrimage to the Shrine of the Immaculate Conception at Seez. The mother wrote to Mrs. Guerin at this time: "Leonie will make her First Holy Communion on Trinity Sunday. She knows her catechism perfectly, and answers my questions better than I would have believed possible."

But the mother was not counting too much on this improvement, for she added with great discernment: "But when she tells us, as she does every day, that she will become a Poor Clare nun, I have as much confidence in that as if Therese should say it to me." (Therese was then two years old.)

There was no doubt that Leonie did make an effort, and the joy of the great day of her First Holy Communion was unclouded.

Yet, the unstable character was not permanently changed for the better, and she was a source of continual anxiety to her parents. Her disposition contrasted strangely with that of her sisters who gave their parents nothing but consolation. Leonie's history recalls these words of St. Therese: "There are some souls for whom God waits in patient mercy, giving His light and strength by degrees."

Under her disturbing exterior, however, Leonie had a heart rich in affection and capable of great sacrifice for others. In 1875, when she was twelve, she was invited by her uncle and aunt (Mr. and Mrs. Guerin) to visit them in Lisieux, but for a long time she refused to go. Her mother long afterwards discovered that her refusal was a pure act of unselfishness. Leonie had thought that if she went, Celine could not go. The mother reports this discovery in this letter to Mrs. Guerin: "We hear nothing from the children but talk of the visit to Lisieux, even from the baby Therese who wants to see Celine's godmother [Mrs. Guerin] and your baby Jeanne. Leonie says to Therese: 'I will give you, dear, to bring to Jeanne, all the cakes given to me. I won't eat one myself!' Poor Leonie has a good heart and loves her little sisters, Therese and Celine, very much. I have discovered that the reason she did not want to visit you was that she thought that if she went, Celine could not go."

This letter recalls a passage from the *Autobiography* in which St. Therese wrote: "My dear Leonie held a very warm place in my heart. She loved me very much and her love was returned. In the evening when she came home from school, she used to take care of me while the others were out walking. I can still hear the sweet lullabies that she sang to me in her sweet voice to put me to sleep."

St. Therese also tells us in her *Autobiography* of the generosity of Leonie in offering to her little sisters a basket filled with dolls, doll clothes, pretty pieces of cloth and other childish treasures. This offering demonstrates the heart of gold of Leonie, who could never see her sisters admire an object belonging to her without offering it to them spontaneously.

Her mother recognized her good heart and also her strong will which, however, had not yet been oriented towards its true goal. The spirit of contradiction seemed inborn in Leonie. At times she gave the impression of shutting herself in, barricading herself in her sullenness. After meals, she withdrew from the family recreations, remaining in the kitchen with the maid, Louise, who seemed to exercise a strange fascination over her. However, she would return to her mother by fits and starts, and practice unlooked-for acts of unselfishness.

A mystery, only cleared up later, seemed to hang about Leonie, and for her parents she constituted a living enigma. Her mother was not discouraged. She noted the slightest signs of improvement; she entrusted the child to Marie's special care, and the latter, who had finished school, gained the happiest influence over her. She would appeal to her heart and hopefully note the successes obtained, precarious though these might be.

Some extracts from the mother's correspondence show her at different stages, exercising the art of the educator at work on this unpromising material. In September, 1875, she wrote:

"I am not displeased with my Leonie. If only one could succeed in getting the better of her stubbornness, and rendering her character more flexible, we could make her a good daughter, devoted and not afraid to spend herself. She has a will of iron. When she wants something, she triumphs over every obstacle in order to gain her ends. But she is not at all religious. She says her prayers only when she cannot do otherwise. This afternoon, I made her come to me to read a few prayers, but she soon had enough and said: 'Mama, tell me the life of Our Lord Jesus Christ.' I was not prepared to tell stories. It tires me greatly, and I have always a sore throat. However I made an effort, and told her of the life of Our Lord. When I came to the Passion, her tears burst forth.

"As I write, Leonie has come down to bring me her rosary and says: 'Do you love me, Mama? I will not disobey you again.' At times, she has good moments and makes good resolutions, but they do not last."

Mrs. Martin's "Errands"

Leonie's instability all but discouraged her mother who, sensing the approach of her own death, asked herself what in that event would become of Leonie. She confided her worries especially to her Visitation sister, and during their last visit in January, 1877, she begged her sister, who was near death, to interest herself in Leonie in heaven. Mrs. Martin almost playfully reports to Pauline this visit:

"Here are the errands I gave my sister to do in heaven. Go to the Blessed Virgin and say to her: 'My good Mother, you have played a trick on my sister in giving her that poor Leonie. She is not the kind of child she asked of you. It is necessary to repair that mistake.'

"Then go to find Blessed Margaret Mary and say to her: 'Why did you cure Leonie miraculously? It would have been better to let her die. You are bound in conscience to set things right.'

"My sister reproached me for speaking like that, but I had no bad intention, as God knows. Maybe, though, I did wrong and maybe I won't be heard."

But her messages probably reached heaven before her sister's arrival, if one can judge from this letter Mrs. Martin wrote ten days after to Mrs. Guerin:

"Yesterday Leonie said to Marie, 'I want to write to my aunt [Sister Marie-Dosithee] before she dies to give her my messages for heaven. I want her to ask the good God to give me a religious vocation.' Marie pretended to scoff at the idea just to see what Leonie would do, but Leonie persisted, saying: 'If all the world were to scoff at me, it's all the same to me; that's what I want to say to my aunt before she dies.'

"Today she wrote her letter, all by herself, without anyone saying one word to her to give her any ideas. Here is what she wrote: 'My dear Aunt: I keep like a relic the holy picture you gave me. I look at it every day, as you told me, and pray to become obedient. Marie had it framed for me. My dear Aunt, when you get to heaven, will you please ask the good God, if He pleases, to give me the grace to be converted and also to give me the vocation of becoming a true religious, for I think of that every day. I beg of you, do not forget my little errand, for I am sure the good God will hear you. Good-bye, my dear Aunt, I embrace you with all my heart. Your very affectionate niece, Leonie.'

"What do you think of that? I myself was astonished. Where did she get such ideas? Certainly not from me. I didn't put the idea into her head, for I was even convinced that, barring a miracle, Leonie would never enter religious life.

"I assure you that her little letter revived my courage, and I am inspired to hope that perhaps God has His merciful plans for that child. If the sacrifice of my life is all that is necessary that Leonie become a saint, I would offer it cheerfully."

Reporting the same event to Pauline, then a student at the Visitation at Mans, the mother wrote: "This evening I said to Marie: 'There is one thing that astounds me. That is that Leonie wrote the phrase "a true religious." ' Marie answered, 'I was surprised too. I insisted that she erase "true," but Leonie was just as insistent in retaining it, saying, "I beg of you, let it stay. I mean just that.' ' The next day Marie asked Leonie: 'What does "true religious" mean?' Leonie replied: 'It means that I wish to be a religious who is altogether good, in fact, a saint.' "

But in spite of Leonie's evident good will, sainthood was a long way off, as the mother's next letter shows:

"Yesterday Leonie had an odious day. At mid-day I told her to make some sacrifices to overcome her bad humor and that at each victory she was to go and put a counter in a drawer, and that we should count them up at night. She was pleased at that, but there were no counters! So I made her bring me a cork, which I cut in seven little disks.

"In the evening I asked her how many 'victories' she could show me. There were none. She had been at her worst. I was displeased and spoke to her severely, telling her that it did not become her to talk about being a nun under these present conditions.

"Then came tears and she was really sorry. She flooded my face with her tears, and today there are already some disks in the drawer."

One thought upheld Mrs. Martin in the task of educating Leonie, a task which seemed always to be commenced over again: the child of so many prayers and so much sorrow could not perish! And then, had not Sister Marie-Dosithee, whose supernatural intuitions came near to being prophecies, said of Leonie, "I cannot help thinking that, sooner or later, this child will be a Visitation nun"?

Death of Leonie's Aunt and a Mystery Solved

Several weeks after Leonie wrote her letter to her aunt, the latter died, February 24, 1877. Our Lord did not delay in sending proof that the holy aunt had not forgotten the "commissions" and "errands" entrusted to her. For, shortly after the aunt's death, a providential incident uncovered the violent pressure exerted on Leonie by one of the Martin's domestics, Louise.

Three weeks after the aunt's death, Marie began to notice that Leonie, although she systematically sulked over her mother's orders, would blindly obey the least injunction of the servant, Louise. In vain did Mrs. Martin bid her to come out with her or share her sisters' recreations after meals. But then Marie, puzzled by snatches of conversation she had overheard, had been watching more closely the relations between the child and the maid. She watched, she questioned, she forced avowals; in short, she discovered the secret.

Faithful to death, but of a violent character and utterly lacking in any notion of moral training, Louise had prided herself upon being able to rule the girl over whom nobody else could gain any influence. She made use of her domineering manner and literally terrified Leonie, who became her slave, beaten and content to be so. Louise in her devotion to the family desired only to conquer the child's difficult character but, instead, she terrorized Leonie and, unconsciously perhaps, succeeded only in increasing her spirit of disobedience towards her parents. Leonie must obey her unquestioningly, but her alone, on pain of a punishment she would remember. The intrigue had been carried on in so underhanded a way that the mother had been unable to discover it. In vain had she made every effort to gain her daughter's confidence. The latter had been forbidden by Louise to speak out. What such a system had made of a nature already difficult may be imagined. Before long Leonie had become a hypocrite and a rebel.

It is easy to picture Mrs. Martin's indignation at this sudden revelation. She had nothing with

The Little Flower with her Mother.

which to reproach herself. Overwhelmed with work and cares, she had been obliged to leave considerable initiative to the maid who was, moreover, capability personified and apparently worthy of every confidence. The reaction was not less violent for that. So loving by nature, this mother recoiled with her whole soul from a system of constraint that encouraged rebellion under pretext of breaking down resistance. Mrs. Martin declared: "Brutality never reformed anyone; it only makes slaves, and that is what has happened to this poor child."

The sudden change was to be complete. Mrs. Martin explains in a letter of March 12th, 1877, to Pauline:

"I believe I have obtained a great grace through your aunt's prayers. I have so often recommended poor Leonie to her since she went to heaven, that I believe I am experiencing the effects of my prayers.

"You know what your sister was like: a model of insubordination, having never obeyed me except when forced to do so. In a spirit of contradiction, she would do the precise contrary of what I wished, even when she would have wished to do the thing asked of her. In short, she obeyed only the maid.

"I have tried by every means in my power to win her. Everything had failed up to this day, and it was the greatest sorrow I have ever had in my life. Since your aunt died, I have implored her to win the heart of this child for me, and on Sunday morning I was heard. I now possess Leonie completely. She will no longer leave me for a moment, kisses me till she nearly stifles me, does anything I bid her without question, and works beside me all day long.

"The maid has entirely lost her authority and it is certain that she will never again have any ascendency over Leonie. She, the servant, wept and moaned when I told her to leave immediately, but I no longer wished to have her in my sight. She has so besought me to let her remain, that I am going to wait a little yet, but she is forbidden to address a word to Leonie. I am now treating the child so gently that, little by little, I hope to succeed in correcting her faults.*

---

* The servant Louise had been with the Martin family eleven years. When Louise was ill, Mrs. Martin nursed her as she would one of her own children. For three weeks she was at the servant's bedside day and night. In spite of her dismissal after Mrs. Martin's death, the faithful Louise never forgot Mrs. Martin's kindness and in 1923, several months before she died, Louise wrote to Pauline: "In my sufferings, I invoke my little Therese and her good and holy mother; for if little Therese is a saint, then, in my opinion, her mother is one also and a great one."

"Yesterday she came for a walk with me and we went to the Poor Clares. She whispered to me, 'Mother, ask the cloistered nuns to pray for me that I may be a nun.' In short, all is going well; let us hope that it will last."

Re-education and Readjustment

The obstacle that had barred all access to this soul having been removed, it was necessary to re-educate the child, and Mrs. Martin undertook the task with the ardor of youth. All the principles that had guided her in the training of her other children she now applied with complete success. Never had she showed so much patience, so much gentleness. Some accused her of overdoing it; she did not care. Her husband and she had very decided opinions on the subject. Capricious and turbulent the girl remained. She would sometimes quarrel with her sisters and lose control of herself. But the main victory was that she ceased to be shut into herself; she made sacrifices; she wished to please her parents and, still more, to please God. She was "readjusted"; the rest would come in time. The mother is triumphant when she can write of her daughter on May 10, 1877:

"She loves me as much as anyone could, and with this love, that of God is penetrating her heart. She has unlimited trust in me, and goes so far as to tell me her slightest misdoings. She really wants to change her life, and is making many efforts that I can appreciate as no one else can.

"I cannot help thinking that this transformation is due to the prayers of my saintly sister, for all was altered two or three weeks after her death. It is she also who has obtained for me the grace to know how to act so as to win Leonie's affection, and I hope God will let me finish my task which is far from completed as yet. It takes time to conquer such a nature, and I see that this mission has been entrusted to me and that no other could fulfil it, not even the religious of the Visitation. They would send the child away, as they have already done."

To cultivate this "ungrateful soil," as she once called it, Mrs. Martin, whose health continued to fail, asked of Heaven a respite. No one understood a mother's work as she did, and this task, glorious beyond all others in its humility, she now felt she must continue with this daughter who had suffered from "a bad start."

On March 22, 1897, she wrote to Pauline: "It is for this that I feel at present a longing to live such as I have not felt hitherto. I am very necessary to this child. After I am gone she will be too unhappy and no one will be able to make her obey saving the woman who has victimized her. But no! that she shall not do, for as soon as I am dead, she must leave at once. I believe they will not refuse to carry out this my last wish. But I am trusting in God and I am now asking Him the grace to live. I am quite willing that He should not take away my disease and that I should die of it, but I beseech Him to leave me long enough here so that Leonie may no longer need me."

The Pilgrimage to Lourdes

With this in mind, the mother in June, 1877, made a pilgrimage to Lourdes, taking Marie, Pauline and Leonie with her. The mother herself, as she well knew, was suffering from an advanced cancer of the breast. But with her usual self-forgetfulness, she sought the intercession of Our Lady in favor of Leonie. She wrote to her sister-in-law: "I shall bring Leonie with me so that if Our Lady does not cure me,

I will beg her to cure my child, to open her intelligence and to make her a saint." She rubbed Leonie's forehead with the Lourdes water, praying that the child might develop and become less introverted. The mother had a kind of intuition that she was heard.

Mrs. Martin's own condition did not improve during or after the pilgrimage to Lourdes, but her resignation was complete, as is evident in this letter written to Pauline at the time:

"Well, I am still waiting for the miracle of God's loving kindness and omnipotence through the intercession of His Blessed Mother. Not that I ask Him to take away my disease altogether, but only to spare me a few more years of life, in order that I may have time to bring up my children, and especially poor Leonie, who needs me so much and for whom I am so sorry.

"She is less favored than you others as regards natural endowments but, nevertheless, she has a heart that yearns to love and be loved, and only a mother can show her at every moment the affection she craves, and observe her closely enough to benefit her.

"The dear child shows me unbounded tenderness; she anticipates my wishes; nothing she does for me costs her anything; she watches me closely to find out what will please me; she is almost too anxious about it.

"But as soon as the others ask anything of her, her face clouds over, her expression changes in an instant. Gradually I am succeeding in making her overcome this, though she still forgets very often."

In the mysterious designs of Providence, Mrs. Martin was to complete her education of Leonie from heaven. Her condition became such that there was no hope left. But with complete serenity, this heroic Christian mother submitted to God's will. She even forced herself to be gay with the family to bolster their courage, as is evident in this letter to Pauline, written the month before the mother died:

"Leonie read in the *Semaine Religieuse* of a holy soul who offered her life for the Pope and who was heard. Now Leonie wants to die in my place and is making a novena for that purpose. Thursday morning she said to Marie: 'I am going to die; I don't feel well; God has heard my prayer.' Marie laughed at her, but that made Leonie, who was entirely serious about it, cry. Fifteen minutes later, her tears had dried and, with her volatile spirit, she had other things in mind and told us that she had to have a pair of tapestry slippers. I said to her: 'But since you want to die, that would be a waste of money.' She was silent, hoping perhaps that she would be given time to use the slippers. Perhaps she put the slippers amongst her stipulations in her prayers to die, and perhaps she promised to make them last a long time by wearing them only on big feast days."

With such self-mastery, fulfilling all her responsibilities, despite her suffering, Mrs. Martin remained to the end the soul of her family circle.

Almost on the eve of her death, Mrs. Martin, thinking anxiously of Leonie, said to Marie: "Who will take care of poor Leonie when I am gone? That is not your father's role, good as he is. Who will love her as a mother?"

Marie replied: "I will, Mama. I promise you."

In telling this later to Mrs. Guerin, Marie said: "But I am counting more on the protection of my holy mother than on my own feeble efforts. She, from heaven, will transform my little sister."

Marie was right. The mother died on August 28, 1877. Mrs. Martin's maternal activity was afterwards so evident that Leonie immediately became a source of consolation to her father and sisters. The memory of her troublesome childhood became a grace, for it produced in Leonie's soul a profound humility. Much space has been given to the earlier years of Leonie, to encourage parents who have problem children who are backward and difficult to mold. It is encouraging to know that such children come even into the best of families. It is also encouraging to know that these problem children, properly understood and guided, may, as we shall see, finally become a credit and an honor to their families.

CHAPTER THREE

ADOLESCENCE, FROM THE AGE OF FOURTEEN TO EIGHTEEN. SPONSOR FOR THERESE. FINISHES SCHOOL.

After the death of his holy companion, Mr. Martin wanted his five orphans to be under the care of their devoted aunt, Mrs. Guerin, who lived in Lisieux. Therefore the Martins moved from Alencon to Lisieux. There they lived near the Guerins in a home called "Les Buissonnets," the English translation of which would be "The Elms."

Leonie, together with Celine, was immediately sent in January, 1878, to school at the Benedictine Convent in Lisieux. Their little cousins, Jeanne and Marie Guerin, attended the same school. Leonie could not of course entirely make up for her neglect of study and for the time lost in the preceding years, but she did well. Any little deficiency was more than redeemed by her qualities of heart and her goodness, which impressed her teachers, and one of them reported: "I was astonished at the delicacy of her thoughts expressed in the French composition classes."

Leonie's improvement was a source of great joy to her father, who was prodigal of patience and encouragement in her case. It was evident that her mother's influence was following her from beyond the grave. Marie, who had taken her in hand, expressed her delight. She who had written, "I am hoping more from the protection of my holy mother than from my own poor efforts, to complete from on high the transformation of my poor sister," was able to send to her father this first victory bulletin concerning Leonie soon after the arrival at Lisieux:

"I notice that she has been changing daily for some time. Have you not noticed it, Father? My uncle and aunt already perceive it. I am sure it is our darling mother who is obtaining this grace for us, and I am persuaded that our Leonie will give us some consolation in the future."

The fact was that though the girl's studies remained incomplete, owing to the accumulated delays, her gifts of heart developed wonderfully. At home, if she did not entirely rid herself of her former ungraciousness, for which frequent sick headaches were partly responsible, she

The Little Flower with Her Father

nevertheless became sociable and let herself be carried along by the stream of family cordiality that made the charm of Les Buissonnets.

In her *Autobiography* St. Therese depicts for us the intimacy of the evenings when all the family were united under the family lamp, their venerable father, like a veritable patriarch, holding on his knees Therese, while supervising the home-work of his "good Leonie," as he used to call her.

In 1881 Leonie was graduated from the Benedictine school and returned home to share more completely the sweet family life at Buissonnets. Two years later, Leonie shared the deep affliction of the family during the mysterious illness of Therese. We know from the *Autobiography* what tender care Leonie bestowed upon Therese during those days of sorrow. On May 13, 1883, when Leonie and Celine were watching at the bedside of Therese, the little girl called out for Marie but, when Marie came, Therese did not recognize her. Marie, wishing to try an experiment, whispered to Leonie and went into the garden. Leonie then carried Therese to the window from where she could see Marie holding out her arms to her and calling her. All was in vain; Therese still did not recognize Marie. It was then that the three sisters knelt at the bedside of Therese, before the statue of Mary, begging her to intervene.

Of this event I spoke to Leonie in 1926 and when I asked her, "Did you actually see the statue become animated and smile upon Therese, curing her?" she replied: "I was there, but I was crying, my hands over my face, and so I did not see the ecstasy of Therese when she was favored with the vision of the Blessed Virgin. But when I looked up, I saw her perfectly cured. Her face had recovered its calm, and no trace of her strange illness ever returned."

Leonie assisted at the First Holy Communion of Therese, and Leonie testified later at the Process: "Therese prepared herself for her First Communion with extraordinary fervor, multiplying especially her little sacrifices and acts of love of God. I had occasion to see her during her preparatory retreat and I found her in a state of profound recollection and entirely penetrated with awareness of the approaching coming of Our Lord to her. On the day of her First Communion, her heavenly and angelic expression showed that she was more in heaven than on earth."

Leonie Chosen as the Sponsor of Therese at Confirmation

But a little later Leonie was to have a more precious privilege, for she was chosen to be the sponsor of Therese at the latter's Confirmation. As Therese writes in her *Autobiography*: "It was my dear Leonie who acted as my sponsor that day. Leonie was so impressed that she could not withhold her tears during the ceremony." This privilege was ever after a source of great consolation to Leonie who, at the Process, testified as follows concerning the event: "My sister Therese received the Sacrament of Confirmation on June 14, 1884. I was in a position to know better than any other her piety on that day, for I had the honor to be her sponsor. I followed her to the altar, holding my hand on her shoulder. Ordinarily at her age [eleven] a child does not understand the full import of that Sacrament. But Therese was fully aware of the great mystery taking place in her soul. I was not able to contain my emotions in accompanying this blessed child to the altar that day."

In all her testimony at the Process, Leonie while glorifying St. Therese impressed all with her own modesty. For instance during the Process she gave this testimony: "Therese was completely forgetful of self, always seeking to give pleasure to others. I was very touched personally by the great delicacy of feeling in her behavior towards me. I was then twenty-three and she only thirteen, but I was very backward in my studies. My little sister used to teach me, using great charity and exquisite tact so as to avoid humiliating me."

Citing another example of the charity of Therese, Leonie testified: "Therese shrank from nothing; she kissed and fondled poor little children, even though they were dirty."

This charity, which Leonie thus praises in Therese, Leonie herself practised. Her sisters cherish the memory of an old woman who was dying not far from Buissonnets. Leonie visited her, washed her ears in which vermin had accumulated, changed her garments, cleaned her hovel, comforted and cheered her with her advice, and, when she was dead, prepared her body for burial.

Yet, in spite of these neighborly acts of charity, Leonie remained somewhat introverted and given to isolating herself. This was true even while, after her mother's death, Leonie's temperament was beginning to be more sociable, and while she was taking an ever-increasing part in family life. Her tendency to solitude was in part the result of the death of the sister (Helene) who was closer to Leonie's age than the others. Pauline and Marie were approximately of the same age, Marie less than two years older than Pauline. Celine and Therese too were natural companions. But Leonie lost her companion, Helene, who died in 1870.

When Leonie lived alone in Buissonnets with her two younger sisters, Celine and Therese (after Marie and Pauline had entered Carmel), the two used to try to draw Leonie into their company and games. Sometimes they succeeded; more often, not. After meals, Leonie usually went to her room and there would inevitably fall asleep. This inspired the two mischievous younger sisters to tease her in a kindly way. One day when "the solitary" was absent, they undertook to transform her room into a monastic cell and pin up on the wall cards bearing austere texts, such as, "Remember death" and "Every time I hear the clock strike, I am that much nearer eternity." But one card, intended particularly to have effect, was less monastic; it read: "When after dinner I do not take my walk, my eyes close to the light of day."

Leonie laughed at this joke, but adhered to her "solitary" habits. When, however, she came to know from experience what it meant to be deprived of the joys of family life, she became, as we shall see, far more sociable. But the wild flower had need of heavy frosts before it would completely open and bloom.

CHAPTER FOUR

TRIES RELIGIOUS LIFE THREE TIMES AND FAILS EACH TIME. FROM THE AGE OF TWENTY-THREE TO THIRTY-FOUR. DEATH OF THERESE.

From her early childhood and in spite of her imperfections, Leonie Martin had had no other ambition for the future than to enter religious life. The years did not enfeeble this attraction, to which we can attribute to some extent her reserve and her taste for solitude. Many times she had accompanied her mother to the meetings of the Franciscan tertiaries at the Poor Clares' convent at Alencon, and she always nourished a secret desire to enter there.

In October, 1886, Marie was to enter the Carmel. The date was fixed for October 15. As Pauline had done, Marie wished first to kneel for the last time at her mother's grave. The whole family went to Alencon on the 7th. It was during this visit that, with a precipitation which nothing had led them to foresee, and of which the future would show the imprudence, Leonie asked and obtained on the spot her admission to the Poor Clares. Faced, so to speak, with the accomplished fact, Mr. Martin consented nobly. He even endeavored by wholly supernatural arguments to mollify his eldest daughter, Marie, who did not hide her displeasure at this unusual haste which, she contended, nothing justified. In fact, on the 1st of December of the same year, Leonie returned home. She had entered, as we have said, on October 7. Her constitution was too weak to stand the mortifications of a particularly austere Rule. With much tact and charity, the father set himself to soften her disappointment.

Urged on, nevertheless, by her keen anxiety to enter the religious life and not being able, on account of her uncertain health, to dream of joining her elder sisters, Pauline and Marie, in Carmel, Leonie turned to the Convent of the Visitation at Caen, where she entered July 16, 1887. After only several months, her health failed, and she returned to her family, who received her with compassion and tenderness.

In her absence at Caen, Mr. Martin, with Celine and Therese, had made their famous pilgrimage to Rome. As they related their memories of the journey to her, Leonie expanded little by little in that affectionate environment.

Then, a great emptiness was created once again in their home by the departure of Therese to the Carmel. On the eve of her going, Leonie, pressing Therese close to her heart, gave her certain counsels intended to put Therese on her guard against disappointments which she herself had experienced. But Divine Wisdom had very different plans for Therese than for Leonie, and the former never once looked back, once she had entered Carmel.

After the departure of his "little queen," Mr. Martin, who considered himself honored to be called upon by God to offer all his children to God, offered *himself* to God, consecrating solely to His glory his remaining years. Heaven immediately accepted his sacrifice, for soon he was stricken ill. He bore his affliction with perfect resignation. During his long trial, Leonie and Celine, his "angel guardians," bestowed upon their father every care and tenderness, while his three other daughters in Carmel enveloped him from afar with loving anxiety and prayers. Celine and Leonie often betook themselves to the grille of Carmel to receive the comfort and advice which they needed.

During this period Celine and Leonie were drawn closer together than ever in perfect and loving union. Of their affection we find evidence in this letter which Leonie wrote to Celine who at the time was visiting Jeanne Guerin: "Just two more days and I will see you again, little well-beloved sister. I miss you much. I can scarcely restrain my tears as I write you. You know how close we are and how much I love you. I am delighted however to know that you are happy and I am always more than ready to arrange that you enjoy the happiness that comes to you from these little visits to the home of our cousin Jeanne."

Then referring to their father, she continues: "The good God may wish to prolong his trial. I think He will prolong it. The best thing we can do is to betake ourselves into the Heart of Jesus, for there alone shall we find the courage to support the sufferings which certainly are not lacking to us. But we shall not weep over it, for we are more than friends of Jesus; we are His spouses in desire. In heaven we shall meet our dear father again, so humiliated now but then to be crowned with glory. Let us be his crown; let us make ourselves worthy of such a father."

In 1890 Celine and Leonie made a pilgrimage to Paray-le-Monial, and there Leonie, who had never lost her desire to enter the convent, begged St. Margaret Mary to obtain for her the grace finally to enter.

Three years later, Celine agreed to become the sole "angel guardian" of their father and permitted Leonie to apply again to the Visitation at Caen, where she entered June 24, 1893. She finished her postulate, and was given the habit and the name, Sister Frances Therese. Celine was present at the cermony, whereas of course her Carmelite sisters were there in spirit. Therese, happy that Leonie was to bear her own name, wrote to her: "Which of the two Thereses will be the most fervent? The one who will be the most humble, the most united to Jesus, the most faithful to make love the motive of all her actions. Let us not permit one opportunity for sacrifice to escape, for every little thing is so vitally important in the religious life."

But in spite of her good will, Leonie was not to persevere. At that time, the Superiors at the Visitation demanded from the younger Sisters complete observance of all the austerities of the Rule, without any of the gradual approaches recognized as prudent or even indispensable in training young religious. As a consequence, several novices of delicate health were obliged to declare themselves incapable of persevering and left, Leonie amongst them. This was in July, 1895.

Upon her return to Lisieux, Leonie had to adjust herself to two great changes: her father had died July 29, 1894, and Celine had entered the convent in September of that same year. Buissonnets was no longer her home. She was invited to come and live with her uncle and aunt, Mr. and Mrs. Guerin, and she was made to feel at home there, for the Guerins had always bestowed almost the same affection and solicitude upon their nieces as upon their own children. Shortly after Leonie's coming, their eldest daughter, Jeanne, married Dr. La Neele,* and their youngest, Marie, entered Carmel. Leonie was therefore adopted as one of their own and filled a void in their home, where she was loved and was in turn a consolation to her aunt and uncle.

---

*In 1926, 1927 and 1930 I had the pleasure of visiting Jeanne Guerin La Neele, the cousin and playmate of St. Therese. The account of my visit with her is told in my "Collected Little Flower Works."—*Author's Note.*

Isador Guerin, the brother of Mrs.
Martin, the Mother of the
Little Flower.

Leonie's four sisters in Carmel followed with compassion the spiritual misadventures of their "exiled sister" and united their prayers to hers. On the day of her profession, Therese, eager that Leonie should share the happiness she was experiencing, offered this prayer: "O Jesus, grant that it be Thy will that Leonie become a Visitation nun, and if she has no vocation, I beg that you give her one. You cannot refuse me that."

Mr. and Mrs. Guerin, through an inheritance chiefly, became very wealthy, and they felt obliged to some extent to live externally according to their means. Therefore they spent their vacations on their summer estate near Evreux. Leonie of course accompanied them and the luxury there caused her a little anxiety, even scruples. She confided these to Therese in a letter written from the Guerin Chateau July 1, 1896:

"If you only knew how much I need to be aided lest I permit myself to be affected by the pleasures and vanities of the world. In spite of all the good will possible, one is unconsciously affected by them, and if there is no sin in that, at least piety and love for Jesus become diminished and decreased. One feels that there is nothing to offer Him. Dear sister, I am weak; I count on you. The memory of you is very sweet and keeps me close to God. I understand perfectly your desire to go soon to lose yourself eternally in Jesus. I also have the same desire. I do not understand those who love this miserable life on earth. As for you, you are ready to go to see the good God; surely you will be well received, but I, alas, I will arrive with empty hands. Nevertheless I have the temerity not to be afraid. Can you understand that? It is incredible, I confess, but I cannot help not fearing Him."

Several days afterwards she wrote Celine, now Sister Genevieve of the Holy Face: "Twenty days more to spend here at the Chateau. I am not sorry, although I have almost the same life here as at Lisieux. More and more I feel the nothingness of everything that must pass. That thought does me good and detaches me a little. But always at the bottom there is sadness that I cannot entirely conquer. For the moment I feel 'Whatever the good God wishes,' but I suffer, and suffer much, for my exile seems long to me, long from the cloister."

The following year, 1897, her exile seemed longer still, when Therese was about to go to

Photo of Mrs. Guerin, Mrs. Martin's sister-in-law, to whom many of the letters in this book are addressed.

her eternal reward. Being powerless to be near Therese, like her Carmelite sisters, Leonie from afar united herself to their grief. She wrote them: "We are on the eve of losing her who has been our joy on this earth. Let us not grieve; let us rather rejoice for and with her. She will be one angel more to protect us from heaven. I envy her happiness, and I cannot pray for her cure. That would be to love my little sister selfishly, and it would be to run counter to the will of God Who must want to pluck immediately for Himself this pure lily."

Leonie's impressions after the death of St. Therese form part of her deposition during the Process: "I saw the body of my sister Therese exposed at the grille of the chapel in Carmel. Her face seemed to me to be of extraordinary beauty. I would have liked to have stopped to contemplate it, but the pressure of the crowd who had come to see her and pray before her prevented that. The crowd filled the chapel, the sanctuary and the altar steps. I heard some one behind me say: 'How beautiful she is! One feels forced to pray not for her but to her.' "

Did Leonie recommend her future to her who had promised to "spend her heaven doing good upon earth"? We can well suppose that she did. In any event, Leonie knew or was soon to know that her sister Therese on the eve of her death had said to Marie: "After my death, I shall make Leonie return to her Visitation and she will remain there."

This prophecy of Therese was kept to the letter; for after her death, the difficulties that had hitherto kept Leonie from persevering were conquered. In the Visitation at Caen changes had taken place. The rigorous Superiors had been succeeded by new Mistresses who believed in a progressive and gradual approach to the rigors of the Rule. Consequently several former postulants asked to return, and amongst them Leonie. She entered January 28, 1899, when she was thirty-six years of age, and this time she persevered. She lived there for forty-two years, until her death on June 16, 1941.

A few days after she entered, Leonie wrote to her Carmelite sisters: "I have entered with a firm step and am resolved, cost what it may, to walk directly ahead. At the moment that I opened the door of the cloister, I threw myself into the arms of our good Mother Superior and said to her: 'I am here for always.' This is my sole ambition: to hide myself like *a humble violet* under the leaves of perfect submission, so that my Superiors can do with me whatever they wish."

CHAPTER FIVE

THE FINAL ENTRANCE OF LEONIE AT THIRTY-SIX. EARLIER YEARS IN RELIGION. CHARACTERISTICS.

Leonie's departure left a void in the Guerin home. Mr. Guerin, who had purposely and prudently prolonged for several months Leonie's sojourn with him, personally accompanied her to the Visitation cloister. The next day Mrs. Guerin, in an affectionate letter, wrote to Leonie: "I saw clearly, my dear little Leonie, that you were suffering much in the world and I myself suffered with you. You have now reached the goal of your desires. May the good God continue to guide your bark until it arrives safely at port. Your years of trial are over; now you commence a new life, a life which you already know in part. Go forward courageously. Count entirely on God. Trust completely in Him. Entrust to Him everything you do. We will help you. Oh, yes, I assure you that in our feeble prayers, Our Lord will often hear your name."

After a rapid postulate of only four months, Leonie received the Visitation habit and was again given the name, Sister Frances Therese, the latter in memory of her little sister in heaven. Leonie lived more and more in the company of Therese, as she assured her sisters in Carmel: "I think unceasingly of Therese. Every moment I summon her to my side. Now I have three angel guardians: the one God gave me, my Visitandine aunt and Therese."

The novitiate passed normally. Her Mistress of Novices found her a very direct, open, simple and humble soul, possessed of a generous will to let herself be molded into a true religious.

Leonie wrote to her sisters in Carmel: "Our Mistress does not spare me. I assure you that she knows how to train natures like mine. Far from being displeased, I am delighted with her strong direction which leads to pure love, and I often say to her: 'I beg of you, Mother, do not spare me; it is nature which cries out and revolts, but at heart I am content.' "

To the same sisters she wrote later: "To win heaven, it is necessary to suffer and to suffer much. Yes, I understand that here below true peace is to be found in the acceptance of the trials we meet at each step. After this time of exile, there will be heaven eternally. Would that I were already there! While waiting, it is necessary to be strongly and lovingly attached to the cross. From the cross to heaven is only a step."

Sometimes memory of the past plunged her into fervent thanksgiving. One August 28, the anniversary of the death of her mother, she wrote to her sister Marie: "This is a sad and a sweet anniversary, and one that reminds me naturally of you. How very many things have happened in those twenty-two years since our dear Mama left us! How many memories press upon my heart! When I think of my childhood and compare the past with the present, I am overwhelmed with thanksgiving to the Heart of Jesus, Who has heaped upon me so much love and Who has hidden me in this very dear vestibule to heaven, where I live and where I will die."

Leonie never seemed surprised when she was corrected, but always frankly acknowledged her deficiencies. She undertook cheerfully whatever humble tasks were assigned to her, and was always the first to smile at her mishaps. She was affectionately attached to her companions and to her Mistress. But her heart was to be bruised a little when this Mistress of Novices was changed and another substituted. The second Mistress was very different in character and had had great success in training novices to be strong and virile in the conquest of their faults. The transition was painful to Leonie who frequently took refuge in tears. In fact, to staunch the possible flow, once she presented herself to the new Mistress armed with two handkerchiefs.

There seems to have been in Leonie a tendency to be slow in adapting herself to the practical details of religious life. This tardiness, together with an exaggerated and too meticulous solicitude about every object confided to her care, furnished ample cause for frequent rebukes from her Mistress. Nevertheless, in spite of repeated humiliations, accepted with sweet humility, the fervent novice lost none of her gaiety. It was her cheerfulness that enlivened the recreation periods. On the other hand she knew how to take a joke if she were the butt of it. For instance, on a feast day, Epiphany, a "free day" was declared, and a good time was had by all. In the evening, Leonie found her bed garnished with no fewer than six hot water bottles, placed there mischievously by her companions who knew Leonie to be habitually chilly. Without manifesting the slightest resentment, Leonie smilingly retained one bottle for herself, and hid the others in the beds of those Sisters who suffered most from the cold.

The novitiate being finished, Leonie was professed, and made her vows on July 2, 1900, the Feast of the Visitation. Beaming under her crown of roses, she seemed transfigured. Was she not the spouse of Jesus, King of Heaven and Earth? In her spirit of thanksgiving she could sing with her sister Therese: "Thou hast made the chords of Thy lyre vibrate and Thy lyre is my heart; therefore I can ever chant the sweetness of Thy mercies."

On this happy occasion, her uncle, Mr. Guerin, rejoicing that "the bark of his Leonie had reached port," wrote to her these lines full of delicate affection: "Many adverse winds have hitherto hindered the progress of your voyage, because God wanted to strengthen and ripen you and render you worthy of the great honor to which you aspire. Doubtless you owe this happy outcome to the graces God showered upon you as a reward for your perseverance. I share your joy, my darling, because I feel that part of the honor redounds upon me and your aunt. For many years, have you not been our daughter? We tried to do our part to bring you to this happy day. Today our mission is terminated. Help us, dear daughter, to thank God with and for you, and believe that your sweet presence is missed terribly by both your aunt and me."

From the Carmel of Lisieux there came to Leonie on the day of her profession affectionate messages from all three of her Carmelite sisters.

Marie wrote: "How shall I express to you what is in my heart for you on the eve of your great day? Tomorrow at nine o'clock we shall surround you with our love and our prayers. Do not believe that we shall be far from you; oh, no, to the soul there is no such thing as distance. Moreover, at your side our dear father and mother will find their places; so too will our dear aunt [Sister Marie-Dosithee] and our Therese with the four little angels [the four Martin children who died in infancy] who preceded her into heaven. Yes, tomorrow all heaven will rejoice. I have placed your crown at the feet of Our Lady (she who, as you know, smiled on Therese at our home). I suspended the crown from her neck and we have all kissed

Photo of Marie Guerin.

it. What happiness it has been for us to do that for you!"

When she received the letter from Marie, Leonie replied: "What a beautiful day it was! Nothing could disturb the perfect calm and peace with which my soul was flooded. Never, never have I been so happy. How our well-beloved little Therese must rejoice in heaven to see my crown placed at the feet of Our Lady! The morning after my profession, when I awoke, it was my great joy to press to my heart my profession cross, that blessed cross that cost me so dear. I say to myself, 'This time I shall keep it.' The cross of which I speak is of silver, studded with relics, and we wear it overtly on our breasts day and night." (After the death of Leonie, the Visitation had the delicate thoughtfulness to send to her Carmelite sisters Leonie's profession crucifix.)

Her cousin, Marie Guerin, now Sister Marie of the Eucharist, also wrote to congratulate Leonie: "Let us praise the Lord Who has showered His mercies upon our family. You are the sixth lily to be consecrated to Him and you are not the least sparkling, since you achieved your vocation by triumphing over so many obstacles. Oh, how completely am I united to you in heart and mind on this beautiful day!"

The Carmel of Lisieux has preserved this letter from Leonie's Superior written to Mother Agnes after Leonie's profession: "I am happy, Reverend and dear Mother, to have occasion to write to you concerning her whom you love with both a sisterly and a maternal love, and whom we also love as a sister and a very dear child. Our dear Sister Frances Therese has been appointed assistant in charge of the refectory. The active work of that office is salutary for her health, which is now really good, and for her religious life, in that it involves constant and meritorious efforts to be exact and to use time well. Not to have a minute to think of oneself cuts short lots of things. Moreover, my dear Mother, the tears of yesteryear have been replaced by a big smile and jolly laugh which gives a joyous note to our recreations. Besides, the ambition to imitate her holy sister Therese in devoting herself to priests exerts a happy influence upon our dear Sister Frances Therese. How very many little sacrifices, so painful to her nature, she accepts in this apostolic role! Your letters from Carmel are also like pious goads which inspire and stimulate her loving heart. I must assure you that we all share both her affectionate veneration for the dear little saint who is the glory of your Community and her respectful affection for her sisters in Carmel."

Of the apostolic spirit, to which the preceding letter refers, there is abundant evidence in the letters of Leonie to Carmel. For instance, in one, she writes shortly after her profession: "How I would love to have the soul of an apostle! The salvation of souls stirs and stimulates me in all my actions. We are religious just for that work."

The Little Mule of the Monastery

Later she writes: "I have been appointed aid to the procurator. I have had that duty for a month now and I like it much. It is my task to put things in order here and there throughout the convent. I regard myself as the little mule of the monastery and I find my lot worthy of envy, for how many opportunities there are for renouncements, for sacrifices known to Jesus alone! How many souls can I save by these little 'nothings,' little things as little as myself! Oh, the souls of priests especially; they are my particular goal."

Later still: "Our King of Love is not known, not loved. That which should occupy us exclusively in this land of exile is to suffer, to compensate Our Lord Who begs love from His creatures. But so very many spurn His love! He deplored that to our St. Margaret Mary. Let us, His spouses, find our joy in consoling Him. I assure you that that is my sole ambition."

In her subsequent community life, Sister Frances Therese was assigned successively various duties. Her orderly and systematic habits, carried almost to extreme at times, were first manifested, as the preceding letter states, in her care of the refectory, where with delicate attention she watched carefully that none of the Sisters lacked anything. But her heart bounded with joy when obedience then called her to the sacristy, where her spirit of faith and ardent love for the Blessed Sacrament would have full expression. Up to and after the age of seventy-three, she retained charge of the altar linens; in her piety she loved to care for the palls, purificators and corporals which had been so near the Sacred Host. She loved also to answer the prayers at Mass and no greater joy could be given her than to reserve to her that privilege.

As the years passed, it became evident that the most salient feature of Leonie's moral character was the virtue of religion. Her love for Holy Mother Church expressed itself in the most profound respect for the representatives of the Church, especially for the Sovereign Pontiff. All ecclesiastics were the object of her veneration and she prayed often for them, loving to repeat these words of St. Therese: "I wish to help to make the souls of priests resemble the angels; to help that they be reborn before going to the altar. To work that miracle, I pray that priests, burning with love of souls, immolate themselves night and day near the tabernacle."

She saw in all her Superiors the reflection of God's will; she bestowed a thousand daughterly attentions upon them; she sought, in all the little details of the duties assigned to her, to carry out perfectly the will of her Superiors. She wrote to Carmel: "I am no longer in the refectory. I have charge of the Community room and of the sewing machine and of the laundry. I am frequently alone with Jesus in my cell, and, to give Him pleasure, I keep my needle going. I think often of my Therese and my solitude delights me. I rely on obedience, which has worked such wonders in me that sometimes I do not recognize myself. I love this virtue more than I can tell, because it leads me to humility, my favorite virtue."

Her virtue of humility we shall have occasion to mention again in connection with the increasing glory throughout the world of St. Therese of the Child Jesus.

CHAPTER SIX

THE ROSE BLOOMS. THE HUMBLE VIOLET HIDES. LEONIE DURING THE YEARS OF THE GLORIFICATION OF THERESE.

This chapter, which will be seen to be more directly Theresian than the others, will, I think, increase our sympathy and love for Leonie. From the first days of her cloistered life, Leonie placed herself in the school of "her Therese" and attributed to her all her progress. On April 9, 1901, she wrote to her sisters in Lisieux: "Today is the anniversary of our little Therese's entrance into Carmel. That memory is the most vivid one engraved on my heart. How angelic her expression was and how simple and dignified her manner! I feel that Our Lord has been working much in my soul since that time, detaching it and making it understand the emptiness and nothingness of all created things. That thought impels my heart to aspire to heavenly things. I compare myself to the little bird ever ready to fly. It is certainly to my Therese that I owe this immense grace."

On another occasion, she expresses the intention of being true to the holy traditions of the family: *"Noblesse oblige,"* she wrote. "I belong to a family of saints and I must not blemish that heritage." And to make speedier headway, she lived in constant union with her little sister. She writes to her sister Celine: "I have been infirmarian for ten days and if you could see how busy I am, it would amuse you not a little. Indeed sometimes I do not recognize myself. But this is my secret: it is my Therese who is the infirmarian; I am only her little aide. You can understand it therefore if I do good work, but it is to her that all the glory belongs."

Almost immediately after the death of Sister Therese, the Little Flower's fame commenced to grow and by 1910, thirteen years after her death, an extraordinary glory already attached to her name. In that year, her Bishop, having received from Rome authority to open the diocesan Process, told Leonie's Superior to have Leonie prepare her "deposition" as an eye-witness of the virtues of St. Therese. Greatly moved by the grandeur and gravity of the task demanded of her, and anxious to omit nothing of importance, Leonie dedicated herself to prayer and recollection in the effort to draw up her declaration.

Distrustful of herself, Leonie who always saw God in her Superiors and always gave to them her filial confidence, sought help from them in writing her deposition. She wrote to her sisters in Carmel: "My Mather Superior has given me the most devoted assistance; so much so that I am moved to tears at her helpfulness. I humbly confess that I would never have been able to complete the task without her help. However as long as I am able to love God with all my heart, and to live humbly in His love, that is enough for me."

Several months later, Leonie was summoned to testify before the Tribunal of Inquiry concerning the virtues of Therese. The Tribunal met at Bayeux, and she was accompanied to that city by her Mother Superior. The modest Leonie, far from being dazzled by the respectful attentions and honors given her, said: "Therese is very active in my soul these days, especially in inspiring in me humility. The higher I see her elevated to honors, the more I feel the necessity of humbling myself. I long to disappear, to be counted as nothing—what a grace to come to me!"

In 1915 the Apostolic Commission appointed to interrogate the four sisters of Therese met in Lisieux. Leonie's ecclesiastical Superiors ordered her to present herself there. One can imagine with what joy Leonie set out for this reunion with her three Carmelite sisters. Up until now Leonie had followed only from afar the successive steps of her sister Therese towards Canonization. Now she was to play a more active part in the Process and in the very convent in which Therese had lived and died.

With a devotion that is scarcely describable, Leonie, admitted to the Carmelite cloister, visited over and over again the places sanctified by the footsteps of her saintly sister. She especially loved to linger in prayer in the cell that Therese had occupied.

Leonie's testimony before the Apostolic Tribunal at that time gives us a picture of the heroic virtue of St. Therese before her entrance into Carmel. Concerning the infancy of Therese, Leonie testified under oath:

"As far as I could observe the life of my little sister, I have never seen in her conduct the least failure of her duties and obligations. When she was six years old, Therese already manifested a great devotion to her neighbor. She did not much like childish games and was inclined to be silent and thoughtful; nevertheless, she would spend entire afternoons at play, contrary to her tastes, to please her little cousin.

"Therese was always very sweet and always complete mistress of herself. I do not remember ever having seen her give signs of impatience, much less of anger. She did not seek sweets like other children; she did not spend the money given to her on superfluities but used it almost exclusively for alms to the poor or for good works or to procure little pleasures for others.

"Her recollected attitude at prayer, her respect and love for religious things, was remarkable from the days of her infancy, while I lived near her. There was nothing affected about this attitude. One could not but rejoice to see this young soul so conscious of the presence of God, her little hands joined, kneeling straight and immobile, whether in church, where she loved to be, or in the evening at the side of our father.

"In obedience Therese was exact, prompt and cheerful. It was never necessary to tell her the same thing twice."

Speaking of the adolescence of St. Therese, Leonie was even more precise:

"She practised the most perfect punctuality in the order of day she imposed upon herself when she was thirteen and fourteen, in order to save time and pursue her studies. She would never argue and it was easy for her to bow to the judgment of others. She sedulously avoided boasting and seemed unaware of the excellences of mind and of the physical beauty with which God endowed her. She says in her notes that she was by nature proud, but she so perfectly ruled her nature that if she had not written it, I would never have guessed it.

"Her progress in virtue was uninterrupted. I noticed in her an amiability and an ease of manner which seemed to me extraordinary. Her continual ambition was not to find happiness here below; she reflected often upon eternity and loved to speak of heaven. She wrote me in January, 1895: 'This thought of the brevity of life gives me courage; it helps me to bear the fatigues of the journey.' "

The reunion for eight days with her sisters, whom Leonie had never expected to see again on earth, was both naturally and supernaturally perfect. "Oh, I am too happy!" Leonie often exclaimed those days. Her three Carmelite sisters and the entire Community surrounded her with every attention and honor. The Carmelites composed little verses for her and about her and reserved for the last day of the reunion a couplet which read: "Dear sister, do not grieve that the hour seems to have struck at which we must say good-bye, for this separation is but of a day and our exile will pass like a dream, and soon, for always, we shall be together in heaven."

Upon her return to the Visitation, Sister Frances Therese resumed her hidden and humble life. Until now there had seemed to be in her an excessive fear of failing, a fear which to some extent paralyzed her spiritual efforts. But now and henceforth she sped rapidly forward towards perfection. She expanded both naturally and spiritually and she penetrated more profoundly into the understanding and practise of "the little way of spiritual childhood."

She cherished in her heart, not without a little sadness, the memory of those charmed and charming hours spent with her sisters at Lisieux. This letter from her to Carmel reveals this note of sadness: "My exile weighs more heavily upon me than formerly; that is inevitable. But on the other hand, what happy memories there are and what stimuli to sanctify myself more and more! O holy Carmel, where I had a glimpse of heaven! God speed the time when we shall be united in heaven, never more to be separated."

She often re-read this letter addressed to her by her Carmelite sister Marie: "Dear Sister: What do you think of the memories you have left us, memories that make me dream of heaven where our reunion will be eternal? Like yourself, I feel the weight of our exile more keenly since your departure. Believe me, there will ever be something lacking in our happiness as long as we are separated. During those days of your presence here, we tasted the sweetness of family joys and relived the life we had together at home in our girlhood. It seemed to me that we had never been separated. Those seventeen years of separation seemed an illusion. I suppose that in heaven when we think of our earthly life, it will appear to us as a dream, 'a night passed in a bad inn.' Yes, truly our life here below is just that, and I feel, as you do, full of courage to climb the mountain of perfection, for I know well that it is Jesus Who will carry me up in His arms, if I place in Him all my trust."

It was during her sojourn in Carmel in 1915 that the photograph of Leonie shown later on page 116 was taken. With her habitual modesty she wrote to her sisters who had sent the photographs to her: "If I did not fear to hurt you, I would have returned to you my photos, for what do you want the Community to do with them? Is it not sufficient for them to have my poor self without having also my picture? Nevertheless I believe you love me although I am not at all lovable. In short, since you like me, I too like myself, but it is nevertheless true that your poor little sister feels herself so inferior to you in all respects."

At the time of her visit to Lisieux in 1915, Leonie was in her fifties, and as she approached her sixtieth year, her health, always precarious, changed notably for the worse and occasioned what was a very heavy cross for her. Until then Leonie had generously given her full and sweet voice to the chanting of the Divine Office in choir, praising Our Lord with all her soul. But increasing age and failing health combined to make it impossible for her to bear the fatigue of the long chants, and therefore she sought and obtained a demotion, and passed from the rank of Choir Sister to that of Lay Sister.

During the chant in chapel she had once been favored by a brief visit from her saintly sister Therese. While at Matins she suddenly saw a luminous hand on her breviary. The manifestation passed as rapidly as lightning, but left Leonie, as she reported to her sisters in Carmel, with the distinct impression of having been visited by her sister Therese. She said to herself: "It is my little Therese, my second guardian angel, who came to excite fervor in me." Leonie was not given to imagining things nor had she any desire for mystic visitations or extraordinary graces, and therefore her sisters at Carmel and the nuns at Caen firmly believed in the genuineness of this brief apparition. The "luminous hand" is not a surprising manifestation, for on the Little Flower's Confirmation Day the hand of Leonie was placed on the shoulder of Therese in testimony of her solemn promises. Now that child, having become a Saint, extended a protecting hand upon her dear Leonie.

In a letter to her sister Pauline, Leonie poured out her regret over the necessity of having had to give up the chanting in choir, and Pauline, with her maternal heart, replied: "Oh, do not permit yourself to grieve, my dear little Leonie. As long as your *heart* chants unceasingly the praises of the good God, all is well. And don't forget the luminous hand of our Therese. This time she has come invisibly to close your breviary, but it is only to open wider your great heart."

Leonie had long cherished the wish that she could possess some notable relic of her "little Therese." Having no power at that time to dispose of the holy remains of their dear sister, her Carmelite sisters nevertheless thought up a way of giving Leonie what she sought. During the second exhumation of the body of Therese, one of her Carmelite sisters, while wrapping the remains of Therese in silk, saw one of her teeth completely detached. "This shall be for Leonie," she immediately said to herself. Shortly after, permission having been obtained, the tooth was sent to Leonie.

As time went on, the world-wide fame of St. Therese attracted to the Visitation at Caen visitors desirous of speaking with her sister Leonie. Often it was necessary to refuse such demands because otherwise the cloistered life of Leonie would be seriously interrupted. For a long time Leonie acted as assistant Sister Portress and, as Portress, Leonie herself often received the visitors who asked to speak with "the sister of St. Therese." Leonie, with great finesse and delicacy, would reply to such requests in the manner best calculated to preserve her own humility.

One day a prelate presented himself at the convent entrance, when Leonie was on duty there, and he asked that he be permitted to speak to "the sister of St. Therese." Leonie replied: "I will ask our Mother Superior, but I do not think that she will give permission." The prelate said: "Oh, but that would be too bad; I would regret that refusal very much." Leonie said: "Nevertheless, Monsieur l'Abbe, I can assure you that you will miss nothing. It would not be worth your while." Astounded at this reply, which seemed to belittle the sister of St. Therese, the prelate retired without saying more. Almost immediately he met the convent chaplain who explained the "deception." Once the prelate possessed the key to the mystery, he was entirely edified and full of admiration for the humility of Leonie who could so discreetly abase herself.

The less Leonie esteemed herself, the more she exalted the talents of her sisters, of whom she was incapable of being the least bit envious. She admired unreservedly everything that came out of the Lisieux Carmel: their publications and their portraits. She had a very particular devotion to the painting of the Holy Face done by her sister Celine. She wrote to Celine: "How can I describe my joy at receiving your beautiful Holy Face! This true portrait of my Jesus is priceless and lives in my heart. In meditating upon Him so humiliated, I accept with more courage my inferiority from which, I admit, I have suffered somewhat and I know what loneliness of heart is. But at present all that rubbish scarcely touches me. What I dream is to efface myself more and more." It was no impractical dream; her life was impregnated with humility.

Leonie during the Triumphant Phases of Her Sister's Canonization

Humbly and modestly but with vibrant enthusiasm, Leonie followed the events associated with the Canonization of her sister Therese. Above all, it was the glory given to God by the ceremonies that rejoiced her heart; she wrote to Carmel: "What immense glory comes to God by it all! That is the best part of it."

With touching delicacy Mother Agnes (Pauline) kept Leonie fully informed and in close touch with events as they developed. The Superiors at the Visitation made every possible effort to celebrate, in their chapel, as worthily as possible, those blessed events.

Leonie wrote to Carmel: "My joy is so great that my feeble heart can scarcely bear it. I would prefer to see from heaven all these glories of our Therese. I said to our Mother Superior: 'I wish I were in a desert. I long to hide myself, to efface myself, to remain unknown, to be counted as nothing.' Mother replied: 'Well, my child, that can wait until tomorrow.' But today, my dear sisters, what honors they give me! I am surrounded with sisterly tenderness, placed at the head table with our Mother Superior, sprinkled with rose petals, and over my head there is the portrait of our little Therese, decorated with flowers."

On another occasion she wrote: "We have experienced many true and holy joys during the ceremonies of Rome and Lisieux celebrating the glory of our little Saint. She has certainly been treated as a queen. But all that, thank God, far from dazzling me, produces in me a homesickness for heaven."

Leonie was sixty-two years old at the time of the Canonization of St. Therese, and one can imagine with what joy and emotion she followed the ceremonies that day in the Visitation Chapel. On this occasion the Visitation Superiors bestowed marked honors upon Leonie, who in turn edified all by the charming simplicity with which she accepted their sisterly felicitations and wiht which she permitted them to crown her with roses.

With characteristic generosity and thoughtfulness, the Carmel of Lisieux (Mother Agnes, of course) arranged that one of the Visitation Sisters (not a cloistered nun, but an "out" Sister) from Caen should go to Rome for the Canonization ceremonies as the representative of Leonie. Leonie commissioned the happy messenger to kiss, in her name, the Pope's slipper. When the Bishop communicated this commission to the Holy Father and asked his permission, Pius XI replied smilingly: "Yes, I permit it, because it is essentially an act of faith."

Cardinal Vico Visits Leonie

On the 28th of September following the Canonization (May 17, 1925), Pius XI sent Cardinal Vico to Lisieux to represent the Holy Father at the ceremonies celebrating the Canonization of St. Therese. Cardinal Vico at that time went from Lisieux to Caen, to visit, in the name of Pius XI, her whom the Cardinal called "Sister Leonie." The Cardinal brought to her, as a souvenir of the twenty-fifth anniversary of her profession, a magnificent portrait of Pius XI, on which was written a special Blessing from him to Leonie. Cardinal Vico was received by the entire Visitation Community in the assembly hall of the convent. There modestly kneeling at the feet of His Eminence, Leonie, deeply moved, answered his questions. Afterwards, the Cardinal went to the convent garden to bless there a statue of St. Therese given to the Visitation by the Carmel of Lisieux.

After these brilliant days, Leonie resumed happily her humble place in the Community with no other dream than that of living a life even more closely united to God. She wrote to her sister Pauline whom she called "little Mother": "Every day I see more clearly that human honors are but vanity. My hidden life satisfies me perfectly. I am occupied in my cell almost exclusively, repairing altar linens, and humming, as I sew, some of the poems of my Therese concerning her little way, which I find increasingly satisfying and increasingly possible for me."

Sister Frances Therese lived habitually with her sainted Sister Therese, whom she called "my dear Directress." She attributed to Therese the grace of accepting her deficiencies more joyously, and she begged Therese to complete her work by freeing her of her remaining imperfections, so that she might realize the truth of the words of Therese: "I look upon all things as useless which do not give me an opportunity to humble myself." To Pauline, Leonie, repeating in part an earlier letter, wrote: "These words of our Therese comfort me, especially on those frequent occasions when I correctly see myself as the least of all people. I have suffered much on account of my inferiority. I have experienced much loneliness of heart. But now I am above such rubbish and have only one dream: to efface myself more and more."

A Radio in the Visitation

In 1937, on the occasion of the solemn blessing of the Basilica of Lisieux by His Eminence Cardinal Pacelli, now Pope Pius XII, then Legate of Pius XI, the Pope expressed his paternal desire that all the living sisters of St. Therese should hear his message, broadcast July 11. Accordingly, receiving sets were installed for the occasion both in the Carmel at Lisieux and in the Visitation at Caen. The day after the glorious feast, Leonie sent to Carmel this echo of her joy:

"Yesterday the radio transported us not only to the ceremonies of the Basilica in Lisieux but also to Rome. What an inexpressible joy to hear our holy and beloved Pontiff, Pius XI! We were all on our knees, deeply moved, especially your poor little sister, who sprinkled the floor with her tears. What will heaven be if even here in this land of exile we can taste such joy! Then that magnificent discourse of the Legate Cardinal Pacelli—and the Litanies—how beautiful it all was! Then in the afternoon the Procession of the Blessed Sacrament, fitting climax to the Eucharistic Congress—how worthily was our dear Jesus praised, exalted, loved, as rarely He has been exalted and loved! How completely this is in accord with the desires of His cloistered spouses! Our blessed and silent cloister helps us to savor such memories."

In August, 1926, Leonie's Mother Superior wrote to the Carmel of Lisieux: "Our well-beloved Sister Frances Therese walks courageously along the road of the interior life, which, she often confides to me, is not the road of consolations but of naked faith. We all love her very much. Her title of 'sister of a Saint' brings her many expressions of affection from all sides, and she receives it all with beautiful humility.

Her prayers are asked by many people everywhere and we observe that her prayers for them have been very efficacious."

Although the fervent Leonie obtained favors for others, she herself does not seem to have received any great abundance of *sensible* manifestations from her little Saint. The only manifestations were the "luminous hand," which we have mentioned, and the sweet and penetrating odor of roses which she sensed on the evening of September 30, 1912, the fifteenth anniversary of the entrance of Therese into heaven. Reporting this to her Carmelite sisters, Leonie wrote: "Since then I am more fervent; this little nothing wishes to become a saint too."

She set herself to realize this desire by remaining a humble pupil in both the Visitation and Theresian "schools." In some notes made after one of her retreats in 1928, we read: "The splendor of the Visitation is to have no splendor. 'Our grandeur is our littleness,' said our Founder. How that delights me! That program corresponds completely to all my desires, to my ideal of perfection. Humility is my only plank of salvation; I love it above all other virtues. I would wish, like my Therese, to become enamored of being forgotten."

CHAPTER SEVEN

HOMESICKNESS FOR HEAVEN. OTHER CHARACTERISTICS AND VIRTUES. HOLY DEATH.

In December, 1930, at the age of sixty-seven, Leonie caught the grippe, which soon developed into pneumonia. Her condition was such that she was given the last Sacraments. She was in transports of joy at the thought of going soon to her true home. She piously kissed her hands purified by the oils of Extreme Unction. Her aspirations of love for God uttered day and night impressed the attending Sisters profoundly. The Holy Father, Pope Pius XI, having been informed that one of the sisters of "the star of his Pontificate" was in danger of death, sent her a telegram giving his Blessing, which filled her cup of happiness to overflowing.

But her hour of deliverance had not yet come. One of the Visitation nuns who had great devotion to St. Therese knelt before her statue praying: "I beg of you, amiable Saint Therese, leave your dear Leonie with us; do not take her away." To Leonie's disappointment, little by little she recovered and gradually acquired strength sufficient to resume her pilgrimage here below.

The Sister who had been Leonie's nurse wrote to the Lisieux Carmel: "You could have no idea of the great edification that our dear Sister Frances Therese gave me during the days of her suffering. How often I had occasion to admire her faith and her love of God! Certainly she does honor to St. Therese whose virtues she reproduces."

During Leonie's illness, His Eminence Cardinal Suhard, then Bishop of Lisieux, visited Leonie and then wrote to Mother Agnes: "I have just come from Caen where I brought my blessing to Sister Frances Therese. The dear invalid is truly in the hands of God. In the brief conversation I had with her, I was greatly edified. It was like an echo of Paradise. It is good to live in that atmosphere."

"Be Sure to Let Him Know"

With her strong spirit of faith, Sister Frances Therese attributed her cure in part to the Blessing telegraphed by the Vicar of Christ. And here we find another proof of Leonie's lovable simplicity, for later in a letter to her Carmelite sisters deploring the "prolongation of my exile," she wrote in the same letter: "I believe it was the Blessing of the Holy Father that kept me on earth. If I should be ill again, I beg of you not to fail to let him know!"

How like ourselves, who in moments of fervor desire "to be dissolved and be with Christ" and to count all earthly things vanity, and yet in less fervent days we cling tenaciously to those same things and plan to strengthen our hold upon them!

The Visitation Community rejoiced when the day came on which the venerable Leonie resumed Community life. Leonie, who had edified them all by her fortitude during her illness, now further edified them by her endurance; for in spite of her advanced age and infirmities, she made the continual effort necessary to follow all the Community exercises. She could not be persuaded to spare herself. She scoffed good-naturedly at her increasingly heavy steps and her ever less agile movements, and she used to hum, in this connection, a gay and mocking refrain with which in former days she had brightened the nuns' recreation periods.

In 1931 Leonie wrote to the Carmel: "I am perfectly reconciled to live on to the end of the world if that is the good pleasure of the good God. It is His will that I love, and I shall consent to see all three of you die before I do, if that is His will. And that, you who know me so well, you will find heroic coming from me, I am sure."

Later she wrote to her sisters: "I have a presentiment that I am coming to the end of my earthly pilgrimage. My soul is on fire with God. Ah, we four, my dear sisters, let us, as spouses of Christ, not fear death which we must undergo to find true life in Him."

Thus, with a common impulse, these four souls, entirely abandoned to God's love, marched in unison towards heaven, supporting and assisting each other to bear the fatigue of the prolonged journey.

Other Characteristics of Leonie

Leonie's recollected attitude at prayer revealed her ardent piety. Her retreats were particularly dear to her. After one retreat, she wrote: "How I love the words, 'The good God operates in us; there is no need to see or feel Him'! Happily for me, that is true, for I always have been and am increasingly a blockhead, a log, and I ask Jesus to set the log on fire with the Spirit of Love."

The Blessed Sacrament was the center of her life. "I would crawl on my hands to the rail rather than miss Holy Communion," she declared. In one letter to Carmel she wrote: "What an immense grace is our daily Communion! What would become of us without Jesus? Life would no longer be bearable. It seems to me that the best preparation for Communion is Communion itself, because Jesus, the God of purity, Himself prepares our heart, His beloved tabernacle." She loved to pray before the Blessed Sacrament in exposition, and often humbly asked that the hours of adoration assigned to her be multiplied.

Leonie and the Rosary

Devoted to the Sacred Heart, she was no less a child of Mary. Going and coming through the cloister, Sister Frances Therese always had her rosary in hand. Night and day she held it firmly. Towards the end of her life, she said: "It is my happiness to sow Hail Marys. In saying the Hail Mary she always emphasized with compunction the words, "Pray for us *sinners.*" She loved to refer to Our Lady as "Mary Immaculate." She declared, "It is Mary who will save us."

Leonie was a true Visitandine. She had the greatest veneration for the two founders of the Visitation, St. Francis de Sales (called their Father) and St. Jane Frances Chantal (called their Mother). When one day Leonie heard one of her companions tell of being tempted to try a more austere Order (as Leonie herself had tried the Poor Clares) she said: "What would become of us if St. Francis had not founded the Visitation! How much gratitude we owe him, and our Mother who so ably seconded him!" The Visitandine, St. Margaret Mary, she regarded as her special benefactor, attributing to her both her cure, in her girlhood, and her zeal in promoting devotion to the Sacred Heart.

When I visited Leonie in 1926, I asked her: "Sister, are you not lonely here sometimes in this convent so far from your other sisters?"

She answered: "No, Father, I am where God wants me to be and I wouldn't be imitating my little sainted sister if I were to be sad in doing God's will. Of course all who leave home are a little lonely sometimes, *n'est-ce pas,* Father? But it is necessary to smile, *n'est-ce pas?* And my little Therese helps me to smile."

I said: "But, Sister, do you not regret sometimes that you did not enter the Carmelite Convent instead of the Visitation Convent? It seems to me that if I had a sister who had become a saint and who had made a convent famous for its sanctity and had three sisters in that convent, I would regret that in my youth I had not entered that convent. Do you not feel that way?"

"No, Father," she replied, "I have no such regrets, because I had no vocation to the Carmelite Convent but one to the Visitation Rule, and instead of regrets I have nothing but gratitude to God for having given me my Visitation vocation which I love."

Concerning Leonie, it will be illuminating to quote here my description of her and further accounts of my visits with her, taken from my *Collected Little Flower Works.* I wrote:

"The personal appearance of Leonie would be utterly unattractive were it not for three redeeming qualities—bright, black eyes full of kindness and amiability, a most attractive and pleasing smile, and a most courteous and charming manner. It was easy to understand why the Little Flower's father always called Leonie 'My good Leonie.' She was goodness and kindness itself, and throughout the interview there was always that willing readiness to do everything she was asked.

"I asked her if she would autograph the picture which had already been autographed by her three sisters. She agreed and I passed the picture to her through the bars of the grille and when she returned the picture she gave me with it a little relic of the Little Flower.

"I then asked her to write a little message, a little spiritual bouquet, in her own handwriting, as a souvenir of my interview of a sister of the Little Flower. She readily agreed and, taking my fountain pen, wrote as follows: 'I shall daily ask my little sainted sister, Saint Therese of the Child Jesus, to bless your mission of promoting devotion to her amongst the Americans.' She signed her religious name, which is 'Sister Frances Therese,' and under it, at my request, she wrote her family name, 'Leonie Martin.' "

In 1927 I spent almost an entire day with Leonie and she was as good and patient and gracious this time as before. We talked chiefly about her mother.

Leonie wrote for me that day the Foreword to my book, *The Little Flower's Mother.* She says in the Foreword, "My opinion is that my mother was truly a saint." I reproduce here Leonie's Foreword in her own handwriting.

Après avoir parlé de ma chère Maman, au Révérend Père, mon opinion à moi, est qu'elle était une vraie sainte.

Sœur Françoise-Thérèse.

During our conversation, the only departure from the subject of the Little Flower's mother happened this way:

I said to Leonie, "Sister, you remember that you told me during my last visit, that St. Therese gives you many favors."

"Yes," she said, "but I never ask her for anything for myself."

"Why not, Sister?" I asked.

"Because she is my sister," she said, not proudly, but so simply that I think it was at that striking remark more than at any other made by her or any of her sisters that I realized fully the close relationship between these nuns of Normandy and their sister in heaven. That simple sentence, "Because she is my sister," I remember more clearly than any other of Leonie's remarks.

Then she added: "And I trust her to obtain for me, her sister, without being asked, all the graces that I need."

"One of her greatest favors to me," she continued, "was the privilege of spending eight days at the convent of Carmel in Lisieux, with Pauline, Marie and Celine. You know, when I had entered the Visitation cloister and they the Carmelite convent, I naturally never thought to see them again on earth. But during the Process of Beatification when the Apostolic Commission was sitting in Lisieux taking depositions from all who knew Therese in life, they called me there for questioning. I was the only one here to be examined; so instead of coming here, they summoned me there and during the questioning *I stayed* in the convent with my sisters for eight days."

Her face simply glowed as she spoke.

"I suppose you were very happy there, Sister," I said.

"It was heaven," she replied.

Leonie read everything new that was published about her sister Therese, and these publications she herself read to other Sisters whose sight was enfeebled. To the sick Sisters she used to read and re-read certain passages from the Life of St. Therese, exclaiming: "You see, hers is not a rose-water sanctity! Hers is true and heroic virtue, is it not so?"

Other favorite reading was the History of the Church, from which she used to cite for her

Sister associates the passages she loved best, and she had a particular liking for the works of Dom Marmion, who developed so clearly the doctrine of our adoption as true children of God.

Above all, Leonie loved to follow the liturgical cycle and the Community learned to expect that, as each Christmas approached, Leonie would not forget to bring to recreation her collection of Christmas anthems.

For Passion-time, she had adopted this short and fervent prayer: "O Adorable Face of Jesus, which will fill the just with joy throughout eternity, bestow upon us Thy Divine Glance . . . ."

The years seemed to take nothing from Leonie's vivacity at recreation. She had a marvellous memory and would never fail to recall to the day the anniversaries of the joys and trials of the Community. She showed a particular benevolence to the new Sisters and was doubly tender to them if she saw them in difficulty. Her manner was always affable and she had a ready smile.

During the war she frequently endeavored to reassure one of the Sisters whose family was continually exposed to danger. "Do not worry,"

Leonie would say convincingly, "you have nothing to fear; our little Therese watches over your dear ones and guards them. Don't be afraid; I have confided your dear ones to her."

"Our Compassionate Sister"

It is marvellous to learn that Leonie, who had been so inconsiderate of others in her youth, was called in her Community "our compassionate Sister." She developed an exceptional aptitude for ministering successfully to the sick, and bestowed upon them the most exquisite and delicate charities. In spite of her fatigue and her own sufferings, she would always volunteer to watch at night over those whose illness caused the Superior anxiety, and up to a very advanced age that duty was always given to her.

One Sister, touched by Leonie's frequent and assiduous care, wrote to Mother Agnes: "Doubtless you know, my good Mother, that Sister Frances Therese has surrounded my old age with multiple and affectionate attentions. She comes regularly to bring me in my wheel chair to the chapel or to the Community assemblies, and always with perfect punctuality and good nature. I ask Our Lord to reward her courage in following all our exercises herself, in spite of her age and feeble health."

Sister Frances Therese brought to her work, whatever it was, perfect application and remarkable solicitude. She placed herself amiably at the disposition of her Superiors. "Sister," she would say, "ask of me whatever you wish. I am always willing and ready to help you." She also bestowed upon her Sister associates thousands of little hidden services, never sparing herself nor counting the cost. As long as she was able to ward off pain from others, her own pain did not count, and her heart was content.

Leonie performed also many duties that were not assigned to her, her purpose being to lighten the duties of the other Sisters. But her kindly meant attentions did not always work out as she planned. She was so watchful carefully to put in place every object that she thought had been forgotten that the other Sisters had to be on guard to place their work just here or there, or they would not find it in the place they left it. Invariably, in that case, the Sister knew well to whom to go to recover it. Nevertheless Leonie, undisturbed, continued to keep everything in order in the house of the Lord.

However, during her annual retreats Leonie would reproach herself for having wandered beyond the duties assigned to her. She would also accuse herself of having wasted time that did not belong to her, a fault which in her eyes was contrary to holy poverty. She loved her vow of poverty and practiced it perfectly. Everything given her for her personal use seemed to her "too good" or "too beautiful." She would accept no particular favors and, even during her illnesses, no delicacies; she desired to live in entirety the Community life. After her death, there was a demand from outside for souvenirs of Leonie, and the Superior was embarrassed to have to avow that Sister Frances Therese had kept nothing of a personal nature in her cell except some well-worn medals, an old penholder and several printed leaflets on which she had written certain notes.

The white-veiled Sisters of the Community would rejoice when Leonie's turn came to help them with the dishes, for they knew that there would be fun. Leonie brought her gaiety with her and they felt at their ease in her company and knew she had a particular affection for them. They knew also that Leonie was especially happy when she was occupied with washing dishes or with other similar humble duties, for she desired only self-effacement. She wrote to the Carmel: "O lovable littleness! I am enamored of it, for it is the shortest and surest way to enter forever into the court of our Blessed King of the humble and of the little."

Final Correspondence with Her Sisters

During her later years it was an ever-increasing consolation to Leonie to correspond with her three Carmelite sisters, all united in following the same ideal of the religious life that St. Therese had led. In their correspondence they encouraged each other to persevere, utilizing to that end all their energies and affections.

For instance, Leonie received this letter from her sister Marie: "I love to know what you are doing. It may be little in appearance, but I myself am doing little things in my office of procurator, with my pears, my apples, my carrots, my beets and my radishes. But in the eyes of God there are no *big* things here below; there are but little things, nothings; even the most magnificent deeds are nothing in His sight. But if, from our little deeds, He sees love shine, they become big indeed in His eyes."

Pauline, Aged 21

Marie, Aged 21

Therese, Aged 13

Celine, Aged 20

Leonie, Aged 32

On another occasion, Marie wrote: "Thank you for your loving letter which gave us much pleasure. What could hold more interest for us than the progress our little Visitandine is making on the way of Love and total Abandon? Yes, she is running along, she flies at full speed —and why? Because she wishes to be, like our Therese, a 'little grain of dust tread upon by the feet of the passing crowd.' Behold, there is the secret of your rapid climb to the summit of the mountain of Love."

Leonie generously accepted the infirmities which increasingly weighed her down, even though she constantly accused herself of cowardice. In February, 1936, she wrote: "I am indeed becoming old, and I am glad of it. I have 'the trembling sickness' and the trembling increases in spite of the medicine and care my Sisters give me. Our dear Mother Superior redoubles her attentions towards her aged child and I do not understand why she is so fearful of losing me, a good-for-nothing like me, a cracked window-pane so easily replaced, a tottering, shaking, old building. Blessed be God. In heaven!"*

---

* When Mr. Martin visited his daughters in Carmel for the last time, he, partially paralyzed, could utter but one phrase in farewell: "In heaven." Thereafter his daughters frequently terminated their letters with these two words.

The last letter written to Leonie by Marie before Marie died (she died January 19, 1940) was received six months before Marie's death. In her adieu, there is revealed an astonishing supernatural and apostolic virility. The letter follows: "They tell me that you are tired out. That is not surprising at your age [*Leonie was seventy-six*]. We shall go together side by side to heaven, and the road is so long that we feel the effects of the journey. Which of us shall enter heaven first? It will probably be I, the most infirm. But I am unwilling to ask anything of the good God, for now more than ever we have opportunities of saving souls. That is worth the pain of remaining here on earth for years more, if He wills it. Adieu, dear little sister; I embrace you tenderly. Have courage. Heaven is at the end of our road. Your loving eldest sister, Marie."*

After Marie's death, Leonie seemed to hasten towards heaven. Her rheumatic condition made it necessary during the winter to transfer her from her cell to the infirmary, from which a window opened onto the chapel, an arrangement which Leonie's pious soul profoundly ap-

* The life of Marie was written by Father Dolan in 1941. It is entitled "Marie, Sister of St. Therese."—*Editor's Note.*

preciated. As always, she found ways of multiplying her delicate attentions to her companions in suffering, forgetting herself in ministering to them. She continued in spite of her condition to follow faithfully the Community exercises. She declared: "Yes, I suffer much, but I don't want to give up, but to keep on until the end."

In April, 1940, Leonie wrote these lines to Carmel: "I feel that I am approaching eternity. What joy! Little sisters, whom I dearly love, I won't be able to write any more. My infirmities are increasing. There is nothing sound in me except my eyes, my heart and my head, thanks be to God! He can take those too, if He wishes. Complete abandonment—that I desire with all my little and poor mind."

Leonie's Seventy-eighth Birthday

During May, 1940, the grippe further enfeebled her. Moreover, her rheumatism caused such deformation that her heart was compressed and as a result she suffered periods of painful suffocation. Seeing her rapidly decline, the Mother Superior, taking advantage of a temporary amelioration in her state of health, decided to give her one last feast day on her seventy-

LEONIE AT THIRTY-TWO

eighth birthday, June 3, 1941. She placed Leonie at her right in the refectory, and at recreation afterwards songs were sung in Leonie's honor. Two great joys marked that seventy-eighth birthday.

First, from the Carmel of Lisieux there came to Leonie the Papal Blessing which Mother Agnes had obtained for her the preceding year on the occasion of the fortieth anniversary of her religious profession and which had not been delivered until then because of the war. The Blessing of the Holy Father read: "We bless with all our heart, on the occasion of the fortieth anniversary of her religious profession, our dear daughter in Christ, Sister Frances Therese of the Visitation of Caen, and through the intercession of her sister, Saint Therese of the Child Jesus, we implore for her the grace of high holiness in fervent humility."

Leonie kissed respectfully the autographed signature of Pius XI whom she loved to call "our Angelic Pastor." A little later she wrote with great emotion, in her trembling hand, the expression of her gratitude to the Holy Father. These were the last lines she wrote. (The Holy Father himself later celebrated a Requiem Mass for the repose of her soul, a soul profoundly

Catholic and profoundly attached to the Holy See.)

The second joy of the birthday was an important message from Lisieux. Mother Agnes had years before given to Leonie the profession crucifix of St. Therese with the understanding that, after her death, the crucifix should be returned to Carmel. Word came to Leonie on her birthday that Mother Agnes had given to the Visitation forever the precious relic, for which she also sent a magnificent reliquary. This gift was a source of great joy to Leonie who had feared that after her death the union of her beloved Visitation and Carmel would be weakened. Pauline knew of Leonie's fear and therefore she wrote Leonie on this occasion: "Have no fear, my little Leonie. If you fly to heaven, I will not fail to communicate often with your Visitation; furthermore, I myself feel the need of such continued intimacy."

That night the Sisters assembled in the infirmary to sing Leonie's favorite hymns. In the arms of her Mother Superior, Leonie (whom the Sisters called "our Living Relic") beamed with joy. But nothing could rejoice her more than the thought of the happy eternity which she sensed was near. She said: "Let no one be deceived; I seem to be better but I feel dissolution in my entire being; yes, my exile is approaching its end."

Later she said to her Superior: "Mother, do not be disturbed if Our Lord takes me during the night. I am ready. Everything has been given, abandoned." Her conversation henceforth was exclusively about heaven. She seemed to the Sisters to be the living image of the wise virgin who, her lamp filled with oil, awaits the coming of her Spouse. Her confidence and trust were complete; she had not a single worry to disturb her perfect peace. She remarked one day that it seemed to be necessary to suffer much in order to die; and that she believed that she still would have a heavy cross to bear so that she might go directly to heaven as little children do.

Leonie had once expressed this desire in a letter to her Carmelite sisters in which she wrote: "I have become so little that I have the audacity to believe that I will not go to purgatory. I ask my Jesus to prepare me Himself for His coming. I, though a great sinner, can have no fear of the good God. On the contrary, it is my extreme need of Him that gives me such confidence in Him that I dream that when I leave the arms of our beloved Mother, I will fall quite naturally into the arms of Jesus and of my Heavenly Mother. What audacity!"

On June 11, 1941, the eve of the Feast of Corpus Christi, Leonie was very gay at recreation. She kept high feast in her heart for it was on the Feast of Corpus Christi that she was baptized. She read to the Sisters this passage from St. Therese's Act of Offering to Merciful Love: "I cannot receive Holy Communion as often as I desire, but Lord, are You not All-Powerful? Abide in me as Thou dost in the Tabernacle; do not ever separate Yourself from Your little victim." Leonie emphasized these last words, little thinking perhaps that her Communion in the morning would be her Viaticum.

The next morning Leonie commenced to dress at a very early hour; she habitually rose early in the fear of not being ready in time for Holy Communion. Several minutes after she rose, the Sister Infirmarian, coming to assist her in dressing, found her unconscious. The chaplain was called to give her, before Mass, the last Sacraments. Leonie did not speak again.

That afternoon two Sisters arrived from the Lisieux Carmel. They were not of course cloistered nuns but "out" Sisters, called in French

LEONIE IN 1915

Soeurs tourieres. They were sent to bring farewell messages from Leonie's Carmelite sisters. The Bishop gave special permission that they be admitted into the cloister and to the bedside of Leonie, who recognized them and bestowed a last smile upon them.

Leonie's Holy Death

Leonie lived on in painful helplessness for five days. Each evening the chaplain came to renew the last absolution and to lead the recitation of the rosary with the Sisters at her bedside. Each morning after Holy Communion the Mother Superior came to make her thanksgiving in Leonie's company. Leonie unceasingly said her beads on the rosary of her beloved Marie, sent to her after Marie's death. In her other hand she grasped firmly the crucifix of St. Therese, kissing it piously from time to time. The Sisters brought in the statue of the Virgin of the Smile, a facsimile of the one that had cured little Therese. Leonie held out her arms towards the statue, as the Sisters pronounced the words of Therese so familiar to all: "O, Mary, who didst smile upon me in the morning of my life, behold, it is evening now, come and smile upon me once again."

It was indeed evening and a serene end of a life that had achieved serenity in spite of grave obstacles.

Several hours before her death, Leonie, in imitation of St. Therese, stripped the petals from the roses which the two Lisieux Sisters had had the delicacy to pluck in the garden of Carmel to bring to Leonie, and covered her crucifix with the petals. On the evening of June 16, 1941, she visibly failed. In one hand she held her crucifix and rosary, in the other the blessed candle. The Sisters who knelt about her bed redoubled their prayers, invoking St. Therese, and invoking Mary under the titles of "Notre Dame of the Visitation" and "Notre Dame of Mount Carmel."

Suddenly Leonie lifted herself from the torpor in which she had been for several hours and fixed her gaze on the Mother Superior and the two Sisters from the Lisieux Carmel. Her Mother Superior, deeply moved, embraced her once for Pauline and once for Celine. Immediately Leonie's eyes closed and, with one gentle sigh, she passed into eternity. The day was the anniversary of the apparition of the Sacred Heart to the Visitandine, Saint Margaret Mary.

The first prayer the Sisters at her bedside

Left to right, sitting: Isadore Guerin, Mrs. I. Guerin, Leonie Martin. Standing: Marie Guerin, Celine Martin.

then said was the Magnificat, for they felt the need of giving immediate thanks to God for the innumerable graces with which He had loaded this humble soul.

On the Feast of the Sacred Heart, the body of Sister Frances Therese was exposed in the chapel choir to satisfy the general demand of the townspeople. White roses were placed on her coffin, and her expression seemed to reflect the peace and happiness of heaven. A celestial smile dwelt on her lips. Thousands of persons viewed her remains and hundreds asked the Sisters to touch their rosaries to the crucifix of St. Therese which had been placed in the hands of Leonie.

On June 21 the funeral Mass was celebrated in the presence of many prelates and priests. Leonie was buried in the interior crypt of the convent.

In spite of the chaotic conditions in France at that time, the news of Leonie's death was given over the radio and in the French and foreign press. In Rome *L'Osservatore Romano* gave its first page to the death of Leonie. Hundreds of letters of sympathy for her two surviving sisters poured into the Carmel of Lisieux.

Cardinal Suhard, Archbishop of Paris, wrote to Mother Agnes (Pauline):

"I unite myself to the sorrow which has come to you and which you share with the Visitation at Caen. I extend my sympathy to you and to all the Sisters of Carmel, especially to Celine, who mourns 'her Leonie.'

"Sister Frances Therese was truly a flower of holiness which Our Lord has plucked from the garden of the Visitation to place it near that other Flower, or rather two other Flowers (Therese and Marie), who already perfume the garden of heaven.

"Yes, Leonie was a humble *violet* voluntarily escaping the gaze of all, a violet which did not attract attention to itself except by the perfume of the virtues that adorned her life. I knew her well, having met her often during my visits to the Visitation at Caen. Hers was one of those lives which form here below the edifice of holiness, which attract God's blessing, not only on the places where they live but on the entire world.

"Therefore joy must have been joined to your sorrow when this beautiful soul left her exile here on earth. She remains yours as much as when she lived on earth.

"I myself can never forget her kindnesses to me and her generosity in giving me her prayers. I count on her continued and powerful assistance."

Now that our humble "violet" is in heaven near the "Rose of Lisieux," may she spread her perfume upon the Church, upon her holy Order, upon the Order of Carmel, and upon the entire world. "He hath exalted the humble."

Shrine of St. Therese,
Englewood, N. J.
Feast of Corpus Christi, May 27, 1948.